THE NAME

THE NAME

*A History of the Dual-Gendered
Hebrew Name for God*

Mark Sameth

WIPF & STOCK · Eugene, Oregon

THE NAME
A History of the Dual-Gendered Hebrew Name for God

Copyright © 2020 Mark Sameth. All rights reserved. Except for brief quotations in critical publications or reviews, no part of this book may be reproduced in any manner without prior written permission from the publisher. Write: Permissions, Wipf and Stock Publishers, 199 W. 8th Ave., Suite 3, Eugene, OR 97401.

Wipf & Stock
An Imprint of Wipf and Stock Publishers
199 W. 8th Ave., Suite 3
Eugene, OR 97401

www.wipfandstock.com

PAPERBACK ISBN: 978-1-5326-9383-0
HARDCOVER ISBN: 978-1-5326-9384-7
EBOOK ISBN: 978-1-5326-9385-4

Grateful acknowledgment is made for permission to reprint the following material:

Bereishit Rabbah 8:1. Rabbi Dr. David Mevorach Seidenberg, from "Kabbalah and Ecology," Sefaria.org. Used courtesy of a CC BY license, https://creativecommons.org/licenses/by/4.0/. Originally published in David Mevorach Seidenberg, *Kabbalah and Ecology*, Cambridge University Press, 2015.

Gershom Scholem, "The Name of God and the Linguistic Theory of the Kabbala (Part 2)." *Diogenes* 20, no. 80 (December 1972): 164–94. Copyright © 1972 by ICPHS. Republished with permission of the International Council for Philosophy and Humanistic Studies.

Elliot R. Wolfson, "Constructions of the Shekhinah in the Messianic Theosophy of Abraham Cardoso With an Annotated Edition of *Derush ha-Shekhinah*," *Kabbalah: A Journal for the Study of Jewish Mystical Texts* 3 (1998): 11–143; pages 19, 24. Used with permission of the author.

Manufactured in the U.S.A.   01/29/20

To Tali

V'ata nisharnu
m'at may'harbay
u'v'chol zot
Shimcha lo shachachnu

And now we are but remnants,
few left of the many;
and yet despite all this,
we have not forgotten Your Name

—*Tachanun* prayer, from the Jewish
  weekday morning service

Contents

Preface | ix
Notes | xiii

Introduction | 1

1. The Cradle of Civilization Rocked Both Ways: 2700–1400 BCE | 9
2. Out of Egypt: 1400–586 BCE | 17
3. By the Rivers of Babylon: 586 BCE–70 CE | 27
4. The Chain of Transmission: 70–870 CE | 42
5. The Wandering Secret: 870–1492 CE | 50
6. Coming Home: 1492–1948 CE | 78
7. Interpreting THE NAME: Yesterday, Today, and Tomorrow | 94

   Afterword | 107

Endnotes | 117
Bibliography | 147
Index | 157
Index of Quotations from the Hebrew Bible | 171
About the Author | 175

Preface

There are almost eight billion people on the planet now. More than half of them are followers of one of the so-called Abrahamic faiths: Judaism, Christianity, and Islam. That's a lot of people.

And so the claim at the heart of this book is no small claim. It is positively audacious, even in an interpretative tradition like Judaism. My claim is that the God of the ancient Israelites—the God of Abraham, universally referred to in the masculine today—was originally understood to be a dual-gendered, male-female God. Half a lifetime of research and my own spiritual intuition have led me to this belief. My hope is that you will take this journey with me and judge for yourself.

The ancient four-letter personal name of God, YHWH, which many Jews refer to in Hebrew as *HaShem*, meaning THE NAME, or as Bible scholars refer to it, the tetragrammaton, has not with official warrant been pronounced in public for over two thousand years. Along the way, some have guessed that THE NAME might have been pronounced Jehovah or Yahweh. Many more assumed that the pronunciation of THE NAME had been lost forever. But I believe that I have found it and it was hiding in plain sight all these years.

The personal name of God is a cryptogram. The priests of ancient Israel would have read the letters in reverse as *Hu-Hi*, meaning "He-She."

Those who read the Hebrew Bible in a language other than Hebrew are not necessarily even aware that God was once known by a personal name. That's because for thousands of years translators have used the substitute expression "the Lord" rather than attempt to translate or transliterate THE NAME. We'll get to the who, when, and why of that as our story unfolds.

This history is told from the beginning and with the general reader in mind. No knowledge of or background in religious studies is assumed. Technical matter has been placed in endnotes, which the reader is free to dip into, or not. Either way, we will be covering a lot of ground.

Chapter 1 begins with a look at the religions of Mesopotamia and Egypt and the societies in the shadows of which the Israelite religion was to take shape. Chapter 2 chronicles how THE NAME first emerged among a people who may or may not have been the early Israelites, a people known to the ancient Egyptians as the *Shasu* ("wanderers"). Chapter 3 jumps forward in time to the exile of the Israelites in Babylonia, where much of the material of the first five books of the Hebrew Bible (Genesis, Exodus, Leviticus, Numbers, and Deuteronomy) was likely edited and woven together; and we'll see how this work, known in Hebrew as the Torah, both conceals and reveals the dual-gendered secret of THE NAME. Chapter 4 traces how THE NAME was passed down through the generations during the Jews' first eight hundred years of wandering after the destruction of the Second Temple in Jerusalem. Chapter 5 follows THE NAME as it reaches Europe—specifically in Italy, Germany, France, and Spain—and what it meant to various schools of Jewish mystics in those communities. Chapter 6 begins with the expulsion of Jews from Spain in 1492, and then circles back to Israel, where a small band of mystics fleeing Spain dedicated themselves to reuniting THE NAME's male and female aspects. We will also learn about the Jewish communities of Europe, where the secret of THE NAME is taught more and more openly, up through the destruction of these communities in the Holocaust. In chapter 7 we look at the state of religion in our world now and consider what THE NAME might mean to us today and tomorrow. And I will provide evidence suggesting that THE NAME is not far from what most of us believe today. In the afterword I will share how the theory I propose in this book has been proposed before in a work published in the nineteenth century and banned by the Vatican—a work written by the Vatican's own librarian. All translations of the Hebrew Bible are mine unless otherwise noted.

My hope in writing this book is that Jews, Christians, and Muslims will gain a deeper understanding of the roots of their respective religions to which millions (Judaism) and billions (Christianity and Islam, each) claim adherence today; that Hindus (who believe in dual-gendered divinity), Buddhists (whose practice involves cultivation of the awareness of indivisibility), and Taoists (whose religion centers on the interplay of so-called female and male energies) will discover a greater connection between their respective paths and the paths traveled by followers of the three Abrahamic faiths; and that atheists and secular humanists will see uncovered here essential truths that they also struggle to understand, given that we are all human and all our deepest concerns are shared concerns. I hope as well that in the process of reflecting on the long-lost meaning behind THE NAME, we will have an opportunity to reflect on one of humanity's earliest spiritual intuitions regarding a fundamental principle operating at the very heart of existence. Those who came before us were only human. About many things they were wrong. About this, it seems to me, they were more than right.

I am deeply indebted to Meg Thompson of Thompson Literary Agency, who conceived this book and without whom it would not exist. Thanks beyond words to Rabbi Beth Lieberman, my wise editor, gracious colleague, and steadfast friend. I cannot say enough about Sharon Goldinger, my dedicated and diligent copyeditor—any remaining mistakes are mine alone. Deep thanks to Rabbi Lawrence Kushner, Rabbi Dr. Kerry Olitzky, Letty Cottin Pogrebin, and Bonny V. Fetterman for reading an early draft of this book and/or related essays and offering invaluable comments, support, and encouragement. *Un grand merci* to Anne Marie Gassier for her translations from the French. I would be remiss if I did not mention Melissa Flamson, who so ably handled permissions. Finally, I want to share my gratitude to editor Matt Wimer and his colleagues at Wipf and Stock Publishers for so many reasons, not the least of which is their commitment to books of theology.

Notes

Except where otherwise noted, all references to the Hebrew Bible, Mishnah, Babylonian Talmud, Jerusalem Talmud, Bereishit Rabbah, commentary from ibn Ezra, Mishneh Torah, and Moreh BeEtzbah came from Sefaria.org.

The following abbreviations are used for books of the Hebrew Bible and New Testament:

Hebrew Bible:

Chr	Chronicles	Prov	Proverbs
Dan	Daniel	Ps	Psalms
Deut	Deuteronomy	Sam	Samuel
Eccl	Ecclesiastes	Song	Song of Songs
Exod	Exodus		
Gen	Genesis		
Isa	Isaiah		
Jer	Jeremiah		
Lev	Leviticus		
Neh	Nehemiah		
Num	Numbers		

New Testament:

Matt	Matthew

Introduction

How is it even possible that the holy name of God, the four-Hebrew-letter tetragrammaton YHWH, whatever it meant and however it was pronounced, became lost? Let me say up front that I do not believe that THE NAME was ever lost, but more likely hidden by a small circle of priestly elites who kept the secret to themselves. We'll get to the how and why in chapter 2. But first, the official story.

The official story of how and when THE NAME became unpronounceable is found in the Talmud, a compendium of laws, tales, and discussions written down by the rabbis (a class of scholars that arose in the late Second Temple period) over the course of some four hundred years. According to the rabbis of the Talmud, in the early days of Israel, common people pronounced THE NAME in their everyday greetings—certainly until 586 BCE, when the First Temple in Jerusalem was destroyed. Upon the Jews' return from exile in Babylonia, increasingly restrictive prohibitions were said to have been instituted to guard against THE NAME's frivolous or profanatory utterance. A new ruling prohibited the explicit pronunciation of THE NAME by commoners, restricting public expressions to the priests, who were said to have stood before the people, proclaiming THE NAME in a loud voice as they blessed them. In time, the priests began to lower their voices, mumbling THE NAME, allowing it to be drowned out by the Levitical choir so as to conceal it from those unworthy of hearing it. Then, with the death of the High Priest Simon the Just (Shimon ha-Tzaddik, ca. 200 BCE), THE NAME was no longer uttered by his brother priests.[1] When the high priest pronounced it on Yom Kippur, he did so inaudibly.

So how did the Israelites refer to God? Outside the Temple, everyone—priests and commoners alike—would, instead of saying THE NAME, employ the respectful substitute name *Adonai* (Lord). The secret expression of THE NAME was passed on by the Israelite sages to their disciples in Hebrew only once (some say twice) every seven years and was never divulged in commonly spoken Greek.[2] Upon the destruction of the Second Temple in 70 CE, the rabbis no longer permitted THE NAME to be pronounced, other than when being transmitted from master to disciple, by anyone anywhere.[3] Even the substitute *Adonai* had, by that time, become considered by many Jews too holy to be uttered, other than when one was praying or reading scripture aloud in a public gathering. The substitute *HaShem,* meaning THE NAME, became a way for Jews to refer to God in their everyday discourse.

Jehovah

But what about the name Jehovah? How and when did that name arise? Why do some people say that was the way the unpronounceable name of God was pronounced?

The Torah was translated into Greek in Egypt in the third century BCE (the first-ever translation of the Torah, a work known as the Septuagint). In time, if perhaps not at first, the word *Kurios* (Greek for "Lord") was employed by the rabbi-translators as a substitute for THE NAME.[4]

By the fourth century, the Roman Catholic Church was in need of a Latin translation of scripture. In the year 382, Pope Damasus I commissioned Jerome (later Saint Jerome) to create a standard official Latin Bible. This work—which came to be known as the common translation, *versio vulgate,* or Vulgate—continued the by-then time-honored practice of employing the term *Lord* as a substitute for THE NAME. Just as the Greek Bible had used the term *Kurios* (*Kýrios*), the new Latin Bible used the term *Dominus.* Meanwhile, in their public reading of scripture the Jews continued their custom of pronouncing *Adonai* whenever they came to THE NAME. No one was pronouncing—or attempting to pronounce—THE NAME. *Kurios* in Greek, *Dominus* in Latin, and *Adonai* in Hebrew all mean "Lord." It seems that the actual pronunciation of THE NAME had been lost.

Sometime between 600 and 800 CE, academies of Jewish scholars known as Masoretes or "Masters of the Tradition" (*Ba'alei Masorah* in Hebrew) turned their attention to fixing for posterity the pronunciation of the Hebrew text of the Bible as it had come down to them. Hebrew was essentially a consonantal language, and so the Masoretes had to invent symbols—diacritic marks—to indicate the vowels. Those symbols were most often placed underneath the consonants, though sometimes above, to the side, or inside them.

The Masoretes had to decide what to do when they came to THE NAME. Should they, or should they not, write out the four letters of the unpronounceable name? Should they write them out but leave them without vowels? They made an interesting choice: they placed an approximation of the diacritic marks for the word *Adonai* below the consonants of the four letters YHWH as a mnemonic device intended to remind the reader not to attempt to pronounce the ineffable name but rather to say—in accord with the tradition, which by that time was already of very long standing—*Adonai*.[5]

In time (we don't know precisely when), non-Jewish clerics would attempt new translations of the Bible, not from the Greek Septuagint nor from the Latin Vulgate but directly from a Masoretic text. And when one non-Jewish cleric working with the Hebrew text encountered the four letters of THE NAME, he made an understandable mistake: he read the four consonants in combination with the vowels placed beneath them by the Masoretes as a mnemonic for *Adonai*. And so this cleric believed—quite mistakenly—that he had discovered the original pronunciation of THE NAME: Jehovah.

Bible scholars of an earlier generation believed Galatinus (the Franciscan Pietro Galatino) to have been the cleric who introduced the error in his 1516 work *Concerning Secrets of the Universal Truth*

(*De arcanis catholicae veritatis*). But the error appeared much earlier than that in Porchetus de Salvaticis's *Victory against the Jews* (*Victoria contra Judaeos*, 1303), as well as in some editions of the Catalan Dominican friar Raymund Martin's work *Dagger of Faith against the Moors and the Jews* (*Pugio fidei adversus Mauros et Judaeos*, 1278).⁶ Whoever was responsible for the error first, it was, as Robert J. Wilkinson has observed, "hardly an error that needed to be invented, rather an inevitable mistake lying in wait."⁷

Martin Luther perpetuated the error in his 1526 German translation of the Bible, and William Tyndale did the same in his first-ever direct translation of the Bible from Hebrew into English in 1530. Tyndale's translation became the basis for the appearance of *Jehovah* in the influential English King James Bible in the early 1600s. And that's how the pronunciation *Jehovah* took hold.

Yahweh

Among Christians, few questioned the rendering of THE NAME as *Jehovah* until the nineteenth century, when the German Bible critic Heinrich Friedrich Wilhelm Gesenius popularized the hypothesized pronunciation *Yahweh* in his *Hebrew and Aramaic Manual on the Old Testament* (*Hebräisches und Chaldäisches Handwörterbuch über das Alte Testament*). A consensus was never reached in the scholarly community to support this. But *Yahweh* joined *Jehovah* as a second conjectured pronunciation.

Stumbling onto "THE NAME"

So how was it that I first stumbled onto THE NAME? How did I first hit on the idea that ultimately led to the writing of this book: that THE NAME is in fact a cryptogram, standing for a dual-gendered deity, pronounced in reverse?

The rabbinical seminary I attended in New York City in the early 1990s was Hebrew Union College-Jewish Institute of Religion. One of the courses I took there was with Rabbi Lawrence Kushner.

INTRODUCTION

If you don't know the name, he is an important spiritual teacher to many of my generation and a bit of a mischievous character. He seemed to be on a one-rabbi mission to shake things up.

One day he introduced my class to something called the 72 three-letter names of God. I don't think any of us had ever heard of this. As Rabbi Kushner explained, there are three consecutive lines in the Book of Exodus that each contain exactly seventy-two letters in Hebrew.[8] "What are the chances of that?" he asked, receiving blank stares from most of the students. And according to Jewish tradition, Rabbi Kushner went on, rearranging the letters in a particular way will spell out secret names of God.

We all loved Rabbi Kushner. But about this particular teaching of his, let's just say that we were less than utterly convinced. However, he had more to say.

The tradition of name encryption, Rabbi Kushner taught us, is evident as far back as the seventh century BCE with the Book of Jeremiah. Twice in that book, a nonsense word—*Sheshakh*—appears.[9] But by using a Hebrew substitution cipher called *Atbash* (in which the first letter of the Hebrew alphabet is replaced by the last, the second letter of the Hebrew alphabet is replaced by the second to last and so forth), *Sheshakh* becomes Bavel, Hebrew for Babylon. Why would the prophet Jeremiah have wanted to use a code for the word Babylon? He hid this word because in Jeremiah's time the Israelites were fighting a losing war against the Babylonians. And the exact same cipher allows us to make sense of another bit of nonsense, the phrase *Lev Kamai*.[10] The *Atbash* cipher reveals that word to be Kasdim, Hebrew for Chaldeans.

Now we were more convinced.

Rabbi Kushner went on, another cryptograph was historically used for the mezuzah, the piece of parchment inscribed with verses from the Torah affixed to the doorposts of Jewish homes. Among the Ashkenazim (Jews who trace their roots to ancestors who, in medieval times, had settled along Germany's Rhine), a custom arose of inscribing the reverse side of the mezuzah's parchment with the phrase KUZU BMUKSZ KUZU. Don't bother getting a dictionary; those words are not Hebrew. This phrase is an example, Rabbi Kushner taught us, of a one-letter-shift cipher. By replacing each letter in that nonsense phrase with the letter preceding it in the Hebrew alphabet (its so-called back letter), such that the Hebrew letter *kaf* (here transliterated as *K*) becomes the Hebrew letter *yod* (here transliterated as *Y*) and so forth, KUZU BMUKSZ KUZU becomes YHWH ELHYNU YHWH, which is a direct quote from the parchment's main side, meaning "YHWH, our God, YHWH."

Maybe the Jewish scribes really had, from time to time, practiced cryptography.

I grew up in a time when teenagers pored over the Beatles' records, even playing them backward, searching for encrypted messages. Somehow a rumor had gotten started that secrets could be uncovered that way; and once started the rumor was hard to stop. So I had long associated an interest in secret codes with a certain juvenile naïveté. But in Rabbi Kushner's class, I resolved to be more open. And, as I would later learn, the world has a long history of cryptography, the science of hiding information, dating back to ancient times.

In the ancient world, then as now, people had many reasons to want to ensure the confidentiality of a message. Many techniques were developed. A slave owner might shave an enslaved person's head, write an important message on his scalp, wait until his hair grew back in, and then send him off to the intended recipient, who would then shave the slave's head again, uncovering the secret message. Of course, this didn't work very well when the message was urgent. The ancient Greeks devised a tool called a scytale, which they used to encrypt and decrypt messages. Transposition and substitution ciphers were created whereby letters or groups of letters of a word would be substituted for other letters or groups of letters.

I wasn't looking for any particular secret message in the Hebrew Bible. Maybe Jeremiah's secret code was a one off. Who knew? But I was at least open to the possibility that more was hidden in the biblical text than might meet the eye.

INTRODUCTION

That is how I approached text study when, in the spring of 1995, our Bible professor, Dr. S. David Sperling, assigned us a small section from the Second Book of Samuel 12, 1–31 to translate. Dr. Sperling was an ordained rabbi, but he was happy to be known as a philologist. More than anything else, he was a scholar of words and one who demanded extreme rigor and exhaustive research from his students. Before one would dare opine on the meaning of a word of biblical Hebrew in his class, one was expected (with the aid of a concordance) to have looked up every instance of that word's use in the Bible and considered every use of the word in context.

The story Dr. Sperling assigned us to translate is a famous one: the prophet Nathan reproaches King David for having sent one of his soldiers, the husband of a woman the king wanted as his own, to the battlefront to die. I did all the research as assigned. But, inspired by what I had learned in Rabbi Kushner's class, I was also now playing around with the Hebrew, looking for possible clues in the text. And I noticed that in this particular story, David's son Solomon is called, as well, by the name Jedidiah (meaning "God's friend") and that the name Jedidiah, in Hebrew, contains a palindrome, a word that is spelled the same backward and forward (here as yod, dalet, yod, dalet, yod—*yedidi,* meaning "my friend").[11]

I didn't think too much of this until I noticed that the prophet Nathan's name, in Hebrew, is a palindrome (spelled nun, tof, nun). And then that King David's name in Hebrew is also a palindrome (spelled dalet, nun, dalet). Three palindromes in three key names in one story? What, I wondered (as Rabbi Kushner might ask), are the chances of that?

The story we were assigned to translate is about the prophet Nathan confronting King David so that he would repent, change his ways, and reverse the course of his life. And so I found it interesting that at the center of the story, lines 13, 14, 15, and 16 are exactly 16, 15, 14, and 13 words long, respectively. Was that a coincidence? Were the palindromes coincidences? I wasn't sure, but I was now going on the assumption that the Hebrew Bible had a deep connection between form and content. I had found a small light, and I began shining it everywhere.

Forward and backward; backward and forward.

Soon I noticed that Moses's name in Hebrew, when reversed, spells *HaShem*, which, as previously explained, is a traditional Hebrew substitute name for God, literally meaning THE NAME. And then I flipped the four-letter name of God, YHWH, which in Hebrew is spelled yod, heh, vov, heh. The four letters, when reversed, could be vocalized as *hu hi*—the sound equivalents of the Hebrew words for "he" and "she."

Had I stumbled onto something important? It certainly felt that way. At the moment I had just a hunch. Would it hold up, or collapse? I had no idea.

A few years later, in 1998, I made note of my partially formed hypothesis in my rabbinical thesis. But I told no one about it and made a formal request that the seminary hold my thesis from public view for ten years so that I might have time to research it further and see if the Hebrew Bible had sufficient enough supporting evidence to warrant presenting my hypothesis for consideration in the community of rabbis. In time, I had amassed enough evidence to believe that I could share it.

Ten years later I published "Who Is He? He Is She: The Secret Four Letter Name of God" in the *CCAR Journal*, the quarterly publication of the Central Conference of American Rabbis (the rabbinical arm of the Reform Movement). A few years after that, the *New York Times* published an Op-Ed article I had written in which I made the same case.[12] And now here is the book based on the research. I'm excited to be able to finally share it with you.

CHAPTER 1

The Cradle of Civilization Rocked Both Ways: 2700–1400 BCE

A dual-gendered god is so at odds with the image of God we all grew up with that our first reaction may be to dismiss the idea out of hand. To the religious, the thought defies belief. Academics will rightly be skeptical, having in all likelihood heard nothing about it in the academy.

When modern students of the Bible first learn that the ancient Israelites had at one time been polytheistic, they may be surprised but not incredulous. After all, they know that polytheism had, at one time, been the norm.[13] When they learn that some ancient Israelites believed that their masculine God had a female consort—Asherah—once again, they may be surprised, but not incredulous. They know that at one time goddess worship had been the norm.[14]

But that the ancient Israelites might have worshiped a dual-gendered God strikes us as so utterly strange, the concept so utterly unprecedented, that we can be forgiven if we find ourselves unwilling to accept the proposition, no matter how much textual evidence might be marshaled in support of the claim. Indeed, Jews to this day pray to *Avinu Malkenu*, meaning "Our Father Our King." Likewise, Christians pray "Our Father Who Art in Heaven." Muslims refer to Allah as *Huwa*, grammatically "He." It seems beyond the realm of possibility that the ancient Israelites—the people who brought Abrahamic monotheistic religion to the world—could have prayed to a dual-gendered God.

That's why, before we go any further, we need to address this skepticism and feeling that the theory is wrong because it is so unbelievable. Yes, the idea that the Israelites worshiped a dual-gendered god is surprising. But in truth, it would be more surprising if they had not, because in the civilizations surrounding ancient Israel at the time—in both Mesopotamia and in Egypt—belief in dual-gendered deities was, in fact, utterly normative.

Dual-Gendered Gods in Mesopotamia and Egypt

Mesopotamia—literally, the land "between rivers"—has long been called the cradle of civilization. Lying between the Tigris and Euphrates, Mesopotamia was home to the Sumerian, Assyrian, Akkadian, and Babylonian civilizations. Here archaeologists found the earliest evidence of permanent settlements, agriculture, the domestication of animals, and writing.

From as far back as our earliest historical records, beginning around 2700 BCE, and presumably earlier, the religions of Mesopotamia were polytheistic. The names of the deities changed over time as the civilizations of the various peoples who populated the area integrated or gave way one to another. In the Babylonian period, Marduk, the patron god of the city-state Babylon, was elevated to the head of the pantheon.

Marduk was a warrior god, depicted as an expert archer; a thrower of lightning bolts; a sky god who rode across storms in a chariot; a battle-ready fighter; the slayer of the dragon of the primordial sea; and the *bêl bêlim*, or "lord of lords." And yet we have this prayer, which may have been addressed to Marduk's pantheon as a whole but seems, as historian Will Durant put it, "as if uncertain of the sex of the god":[15]

> How long, my god * * *
> How long, my goddess, until thy face be turned toward me?
> How long, known and unknown god, until the anger of
>   thy heart be pacified?
> How long, known and unknown goddess, until thy

unfriendly heart be pacified?

....

My god, my sins are seven times seven; forgive my sons!
My goddess, my sins are seven times seven; forgive my sins!

....

May thy heart, as the heart of a mother who has borne
children, be glad!
As a mother who hath borne children, as a father who hath
begotten (them), may it be glad![16]

The most prominent goddess in the Mesopotamian pantheon at the time was gender-bending Ishtar, the name by which she was known to the Babylonians and Akkadians (originally Inanna, she was Astarte to the Greeks). The goddess of both love and war, she was called by the late Assyriologist/Sumerologist Tikva Frymer-Kensky "the goddess who models the crossing of gender lines." Described as "hero" and "manly," she "transcends gender polarities and is said to turn men into women and women into men." At her festivals "men dress as women and women as men, and cultic dancers wear outfits that are men's clothes on the right, and women's on the left." In her Semitic form, such as Ishtar of the Old Babylonian Agushaya Hymn, she is praised for her *zikrutu*, literally her "manliness." Needless to say "when she marries she never takes on the jobs of wives" such as making cloth and will never "have to perform any of the domestic duties of ordinary wives." "Inanna," Frymer-Kensky declares, "stands at the boundary of differences between man and woman."[17]

To the south, Egypt, as old as the oldest civilizations of Mesopotamia, also worshiped dual-gendered gods. For instance, Hapi—the Egyptian god who personified the annual flooding of the Nile and hence fertility itself—was depicted as an androgyne: male but full-breasted, seemingly pregnant, and wearing a false beard. Not surprisingly perhaps, given this deity's dual nature, Hapi was sometimes depicted as a pair of figures.

Other pairs of gods who appear in Egyptian mythology—such as the so-called Ogdoad of Hermopolis, a group of eight Egyptian deities who appear as four male-female pairs—were also understood to be dual-gendered deities, each of whom could manifest in either male or female form: Naunet and Nu, Amaunet and Amun, Kauket and Kuk, and Huh and Hauhet.

A few hundred years before King Solomon built his Temple to YHWH in Jerusalem, the Pharaoh Akhenaten (1353–1336 BCE)[18] built the city Amarna, which he dedicated to Aten, Egypt's dual-gendered deity whom Akhenaten elevated to supreme god. Scholars continue to debate whether the Aten cult was true monotheism (belief in one god) or rather monolatry (worship of one god). But that the Egyptians believed Aten was of dual gender is not in question. In tomb texts found at Amarna, Aten is referred to as the "mother and father of all creation." And much has been made of the fact that Aten's champion, the Pharaoh Akhenaten, whom inscriptions tell us sired at least six daughters, had himself depicted in artwork as an androgyne, with a decidedly feminine physique.

In enthroning their own dual-gendered God, the ancient Israelites were doing nothing surprising; they were simply following the custom of their time and place. The historical record is clear: the earliest appearance of the first version of THE NAME occurs at the same time dual-gendered deities were being worshiped in Mesopotamia and Egypt.

Why Dual Gender?

A theory of why the ancients believed in dual-gendered gods was put forth by Frymer-Kensky. Frymer-Kensky's theory is sociological; it argues that the reason Mesopotamian gods such as Ninurra and Damu sometimes manifested as male and other times as female had to do with changing societal gender roles. She notes that Ninurra, the goddess of pottery making, appeared at first as the wife of the god Shara (the city god of Umma). But as time went on and the role of pottery making in that society shifted from women to men, Ninurra was transformed into a male god. Similarly, Damu, the goddess of healing, appeared at first as the daughter of Ninisinna (and later as the daughter of Gula). But when the role of healer in the society shifted from women to men, Damu was turned into Gula's son and coworker.

Another way of making sense of dual or hybrid forms is to view them through a political lens. Two city-states forging an alliance would need a way to bring their people under one banner.[19] Honoring their respective patron gods equally would be one way in which the leaders could help foster a sense of oneness in the people. That assumedly was the intent of Pharaoh Narmer—who some scholars believe to have been the pharaoh who united Upper and Lower Egypt—when he displayed images of Bat (the goddess of Upper Egypt) and Horus (the god of Lower Egypt) on what today is called the Palette of Narmer. Hybrid beings (although not necessarily of dual gender) can also be seen in Egypt's evolving mythology. As the seat of power shifted over time, the local deity of the emerging power center would be merged with Egypt's national sun god Ra, their stories and identities combined. Amun became Amun-Ra, Atum became Atum-Ra, and Horus became Ra-Horakhty.

More than that, human beings tend to live in a world of either or. The time of day is either day or night, the season is seedtime or harvest, and people are friends or foes. Somewhere along the line it dawned on someone that the world of the divine had to be a greater, more encompassing world—a world that was not either or, but both and. Could it not be that—maybe on top or on the other side of the highest mountain, beyond the sky, or wherever the spirit world made its home—somewhere it all came together?

The ancients were interested in such questions. Mesopotamia was bounded by two rivers: the Tigris and Euphrates, which at one point merge and run into the sea. How had there come to be freshwater and seawater? The Babylonian creation myth *Enuma Elish* takes up the question.[20] Egypt was bifurcated by one long river, the Nile. How had the world been divided into water and dry land? Egyptian creation myths took up the question.[21] The Sumerians and

Akkadians, two distinct peoples who together inhabited Mesopotamia, were so culturally intertwined that their languages began to merge.[22] How had their separate languages come to be? The legend of *Enmerkar* posits an original, universal language.[23]

The ancients' attempts to answer questions such as these suggests that hybridity—the quality of dual nature—signified something important to them; they saw it as expressing something they sensed as foundational and divine.

Writing arose around 3400 BCE.[24] But archaeologists have uncovered artifacts tens of thousands of years older that attest to a longstanding, ubiquitous human fascination with hybridity. Because the artifacts are so much older than even the earliest writing system, what they meant when they were created will forever be beyond our knowing for certain. But that hybridity was early humanity's symbolic expression for something they sensed as primal is clear.

Late examples of these hybrid artifacts include the so-called *lamassu* and *šēdu* of Akkadia, sculpted architectural figures combining multiple animals with a human head. An example is the Burney Relief (a.k.a. the Queen of the Night relief), a Mesopotamian terra cotta depiction of a goddess with the wings and feet of bird, which dates to the eighteenth or nineteenth century BCE. Hybrid figures adorn the Great Lyre from Mesopotamia, which dates to around 2650–2550 BCE. Probably the world's most famous therianthromorphism, the Great Sphinx of Giza, Egypt—with the head of a human (possibly the pharaoh Khafre) and the body of a lion or cat—dates to around 2650–2480 BCE.[25] Older than that is the Guennol Lioness, a small figure, carved of limestone, depicting a muscle-bound human with fists clenched and pressed, knuckles to knuckles, across its chest, its lion's head turned leftward. This small sculpture was found near present-day Baghdad, Iraq, and is perhaps from 3000 to 2800 BCE.

But hybrid forms much older than that have been found. Some 12,000 years ago, in what is today Ariège in the Dordogne Valley of Southern France, a half-man–half-bison creature, playing a musical instrument, was painted on a wall of the cave of the

Trois-Frères. To the north of Ariège, painted on a wall deep inside a cave in Lascaux, a wounded man is depicted with the head of a bird.[26] The Lascaux cave paintings are thought to have been painted some 15,000 to 17,000 years ago.

Twice as old are the wall paintings of Southern France's Chauvet Cave, which have been dated to 30,000 to 35,000 years ago. Deep in the cave is an image of a hybrid figure, this time with the legs and genitals of a woman and the head of a bison. In *Cave of Forgotten Dreams*, Werner Herzog's 2010 movie about Chauvet, the curator draws a connection between this prehistoric drawing and Pablo Picasso's modernist twentieth-century painting, *The Minotaur*. Primitive and modernist versions of the same arresting image, known to many of us today because it passed, quite famously, through Greek mythology, are separated by some 30,000 years.

But 30,000 years ago, the hybrid was already an ancient form. Fully 10,000 years before the creation of these cave paintings, an extraordinarily gifted (and patient) prehistoric artist spent what is estimated to have been two full months carving, with flint tools, a human-leonine therianthropic figure out of mammoth ivory. Known today as the Lion Man (*Löwenmensch*), the figurine was found in Hohlenstein-Stadel Cave at Hohlenstein Mountain in the Lone Valley (Lonetal) of Swabian Alb, Germany and is on display today at the Ulmer Museum in Ulm, Germany. This 40,000-year-old hybrid icon is one of the world's earliest figurative sculptures.

The Hybrid God

Human fascination with hybridity dates back to prehistoric times. Conceptualizing and depicting divine beings as gender hybrids was a time-honored tradition and utterly normative in the ancient world out of which Israelite culture and belief arose. The Egyptians taught that humans and animals not only had a common ancestor but were in fact one. The Sumerians taught that heaven and earth had been fashioned from the divided carcass of a slain primordial being, Tiamat, and therefore were in fact one. The Hebrews called THE NAME of God "He-She," maintaining that this male-female God, the human beings who were fashioned in God's image, and indeed all aspects of reality were in fact yet one.

But how and when did the ancient Israelites first come to call on their God by THE NAME? That is the subject of the next chapter.

CHAPTER 2

Out of Egypt: 1400–586 BCE

Imagine for a moment the leader of your nation in drag. The ancient Egyptians did not have to imagine it. The myth of the dual-gendered god literally came to life under the reign of Hatshepsut.

The royal Hatshepsut had herself crowned pharaoh following the death of her husband, Pharaoh Tuthmosis II, in 1479 BCE, and she went on to rule for twenty years, often in full kingly regalia, right down to the false beard. She is considered by Egyptologists to have been one of the greatest of pharaohs, establishing trade routes and undertaking major construction projects during her reign. As for her appearance, the bearded and breasted regent Hatshepsut was simply manifesting a quality that Egyptians understood to be fundamental to divinity: the quality of dual gender.

The Egyptians considered their pharaoh god on earth. As the creator of men and women, how therefore could the pharaoh not embody both genders? In time, the Israelites would weave this trope—of the idealized dual-gendered leader—into their own sacred literature: Moses understood God as calling him to the role of Israel's "nursing-father" (Numbers 11:12); later, Mordechai was Esther's "nursing-father" (Esther 2:7); and the future kings of Israel, according to Deutero-Isaiah, would, it was prophesied, be "nursing kings" (Isaiah 49:23).[27]

But we are getting far ahead of the story.

In fifteenth century BCE Egypt, dual-gendered divinity was as we have seen, normative, celebrated by the people, and personified in the pharaoh. It strikes us therefore as no coincidence that, according to Egyptologists, we find in this time and place the earliest recording of THE NAME.

The Earliest Records

The earliest appearance of THE NAME found to date is an archaic three-letter version of the tetragrammaton that shows up in ancient Egyptian records in the early fourteenth century BCE. This trigrammaton is associated with a people the Egyptians referred to as "Shasu."[28] Shasu—literally "a people who move on foot"—was the Egyptian term for foreign nomads or seminomads.

At Soleb—a temple built by Pharaoh Amenhotep III in honor of the god Amun-Ra, in what is today Sudan—"Shasu" appears on a list of foreign places and peoples. A bas-relief inscription found at the temple speaks of "the Shasu of YHW."[29]

Although THE NAME is written here with only three of its four letters, scholars have long agreed that this trigrammaton, or three-letter name for God, is THE NAME in its archaic form. "For half a century," Egyptologist Donald Redford writes, "it has been generally admitted that we have here the tetragrammaton, the name of the Israelite god, 'Yahweh'; and if this be the case, as it undoubtedly is, the passage constitutes a most precious indication of the whereabouts during the late fifteenth century BC of an enclave revering this god."[30]

The late professor of Middle-Eastern cultures and archeologist Anson F. Rainey notes that the Shasu had been captured by Egypt; and he assumes them to be, as does Redford, the people who would later be known as the Israelites.[31] Whether they were or were not the same people, the fact that THE NAME is first identified with nomads or seminomads in southern Palestine is important.[32]

The earliest pre-state Israelites were influenced by the pagans who surrounded and preceded them, although not everyone wishes to acknowledge this. Yehezkel Kaufmann (1889–1963), one of the twentieth century's greatest Bible scholars, claimed not to see any precedents for the Israelite religion in the surrounding pagan cultures. But ideas do not arise in a vacuum. As the late Dead Sea

Scrolls expert Frank Moore Cross writes, "Kaufmann's insistence that Israelite religion was absolutely different from anything the pagan world ever knew violates fundamental postulates of scientific historical method.... [The] epic events [of the Hebrew Bible] and their interpretation were shaped strongly by inherited mythic patterns and language."[33]

YHW was not an Egyptian god. Nor—although the Egyptians absorbed any number of Semitic deities (e.g., Astarte, Anath, and Reshef) into their pantheon—do scholars find any indication that the Egyptians absorbed YHW. Egyptian Jews would later dedicate their temple on the island of Elephantine to YHW.[34]

The original character or profile of YHW (later YHWH) is unknown. Material evidence from the period is lacking. The nineteenth-century Bible scholar Abraham Kuenen theorizes that YHWH had originally been a light or sun god.[35] William Robertson Smith theorizes that YHWH had originally been a storm god, a theory adopted and popularized by Julius Wellhausen.[36]

Based on the story of God's self-revelation to Moses as *Ehyeh Asher Ehyeh*, popularly translated "I Am That I Am" or "I Will Be That Which I Will Be" (Exodus 3:14), some modern scholars favor a god whose character is "the quality of absolute Being."[37]

An abbreviated form, *Ehyeh*, appears in the Book of Hosea, which is set in eighth-century BCE Israel, some six centuries after YHW (later YHWH) is first attested to at Soleb. We have no reason to believe that Hosea's *Ehyeh* or the Book of Exodus's *Ehyeh Asher Ehyeh* indicates the meaning of THE NAME as originally understood. More likely, what we are seeing here is one of the Hebrew Bible's many folk etymologies.[38]

A strikingly different profile is presented in Psalm 29. The psalm is reckoned "probably among the earliest psalms of the Psalter."[39] If that is so, it may provide rare witness to this god's very early mythology. Line 5 of the psalm depicts THE NAME as a stereotypically manly god who causes the cedars of Lebanon to convulse (as in an earthquake), while line 9 depicts THE NAME as if a traditional fertility goddess, causing deer to convulse (as in labor). The suggestion is of a deity of dual gender.

The suggestion should not surprise us. The Egyptians and Mesopotamians had woven belief in a dual-gendered divinity deeply into the fabric of the age. How would it have been possible for ancient nomadic people of the time not to have been influenced by such a widespread belief?

Moving from YHW's profile to origin, I think it reasonable to imagine that, just as the Egyptians likely got the idea of writing from the Sumerians and then went on to invent their own unique, hieroglyphic writing system (as Jared Diamond has surmised), the early people who brought this god to the world got the idea of a dual-gendered deity from their surrounding cultures and then created THE NAME, persona, and mythology of dual-gendered YHW (later YHWH) more or less on their own.[40]

Secret Pronunciation

The Introduction shared the official story told by the rabbis of how and why the pronunciation of THE NAME was said to have been removed from common use, restricted in time to the Temple priests, and then, after the destruction of the Second Temple in 70 CE, ruled impermissible to be said aloud by anyone. I suggested that I do not believe the official story but rather that the utterance of THE NAME had always been reserved to the priestly elite. Now let me tell you why.

In Egypt, the pronunciation of a god's name was just not something the priests would have wanted floating around. Egyptians strongly believed in the magical power of divine names. That belief is attested to in the story "The Name of Ra":

> By the knowledge of his own name did Ra rule, and none but himself knew that secret name. Whosoever could learn the secret, to that one—god or man—would belong the dominion over all the world, and even Ra himself must be in subjection. . . . And Isis spoke again, and her voice was low and soothing, "Tell me thy Name, O divine Father, thy true Name, thy secret Name."[41]

OUT OF EGYPT: 1400–586 BCE

Just as the ancient Israelite belief in dual-gendered divinity likely had its origin in the surrounding cultures, so too would the ancient Israelite priests likely have assimilated the prevailing Egyptian belief regarding the pronunciation of a god's true name. The Israelite priests would have guarded such knowledge zealously. G. H. Parke-Taylor describes Egyptians rituals in *Yahweh: The Divine Name in the Bible*:

> In Egypt, near the beginning of the second millennium BC, powerful curses were directed against foreign enemies. In these Egyptian execration texts of the Middle Kingdom period, curses were inscribed on pottery bowls in which the names of hostile Asiatic princes were specifically mentioned. The ritual smashing of these vessels was more than symbolic. The names of the rebels represented their actuality: the magical potency of the curses was believed to take effect when the bowls bearing their names were smashed. To destroy the names was to destroy the enemy rulers themselves.[42]

Much later, and over a long stretch of history, the rabbis would offer a succession of reasons trying to explain why the true pronunciation of THE NAME should not and could not be shared: THE NAME had begun to be used impiously (during the Second Temple period); knowledge of THE NAME might lead one away from Judaism (in the Christian era, because if God could be a binity, why not a trinity?); and a spiritual seeker needs to find the proper arrangement of the letters on one's own, and so a sage divulging the secret would be doing the spiritual seeker a disservice (in early nineteenth-century Hasidic teaching).[43]

These all make a certain amount of sense. But historically speaking, they are all afterthoughts. The reason THE NAME has not been uttered for all these millennia is because Egyptian belief made pronunciation of a god's true name, outside the circle of initiated priestly elite, unthinkable.

So how did the priests say the original three-letter name YHW? Did the pronunciation change when THE NAME became YHWH? And why the change in spelling?

I'm quite sure that the priests said both the earlier three-letter YHW and the later four-letter YHWH the same way: *Hu-Hi*, meaning "He-She." But to appreciate how that could be, why a change in spelling would have occurred, and why the letters of THE NAME themselves have been held as sacred for all these years, we need to step back and consider THE NAME in the context of the history of written language.

THE NAME was emerging on the world stage at the same time as a groundbreaking linguistic innovation: vowels, which give us the key to understanding the profound magical power the ancient Israelites vested in THE NAME. In the following short section, we deal with some decisions the ancient scribes had to make in light of how language was evolving. This section is a bit technical, but understanding how and why the scribes did what they did is critical to our appreciation of how THE NAME came to be.

How YHW Became YHWH

Five thousand years ago, the ancient world had incredibly complicated writing systems. By around that time, the Sumerian cuneiform and Egyptian hieroglyphic writing systems had advanced to the point where both were attempting to capture sounds, but they still had a long way to go.[44] A much simpler and therefore more highly advanced consonant-letter-based system arose in Phoenicia no later than the late second millennium BCE. This was a vast improvement over the Sumerian and Egyptian systems though still imperfect, as it lacked vowels.

When a writing system lacks vowels, the meaning of words has to be gleaned to some extent from context. For example, imagine seeing the letters *bn* in a sentence and then having to figure out if the intended word was "bun," "ban," "bin," or "Ben." The arrival of vowel letters was, to the ancients, nothing short of magical.

We find the earliest recorded appearance of YHW around 1400 BCE, which is significant because that is close to the time of the appearance of the world's first vowel indicator symbols. (These appeared in Ugarit still some centuries before we find definitive use of Hebrew vowel letters.)[45]

Joel Hoffman, a historian of Hebrew language, in his book *In the Beginning: A Short History of the Hebrew Language*, calls the letters Y, H, and W (in Hebrew yod, heh, and vov) "magic letters." Known to grammarians as *matres lectionis* ("mothers of reading"), the letters function in a dual capacity. On the one hand they act as consonants; but they also act as vowels. When used as vowels, Y (*yod*) made the sound "ee," H (*heh*) made the sound "ah," and W (*vov*) made the sound "u" or "o." Importantly, these dual letters appear for the first time in ancient Semitic texts.[46]

Hoffman subscribes to the theory (first articulated by Judah Halevi and Abraham ibn Ezra) that the "magical" capacity of the letters Y, H, and W to function in dual roles makes them perfect symbols for the Divine.[47] It makes sense. Could it have been simply by sheer chance that the first dual-function letters in history also end up as the three unique letters of THE NAME of God?

Left unaccounted for in the theory articulated by Hoffman, though, is the move from the three-letter name YHW to the four-letter name YHWH. If the Egyptologists are right that YHW is an archaic version of YHWH, and if Hoffman is right that a certain magic was ascribed to the letters Y, H, and W, we still need to account for this change.

Here's how I think that happened.

In the ancient world, the directionality of writing was fluid. Sometimes writing was left to right, other times right to left. Sometimes writing would begin in one direction and then change direction when a new line was reached.[48]

If we think of the YHW trigrammaton not as a word but as what might be called a "lexical icon," we can imagine the scribes wanting to distinguish it—wanting to set THE NAME apart from all other names—with a reading directionality unlike that of any other word. Rather than left to right or right to left, YHW would be read from the inside out, bidirectionally. HW would have been pronounced *HU* ("he"); HY would have been pronounced *HI* ("she").

Beyond setting THE NAME apart graphically as unique, we can imagine another reason the priests would have liked the idea of employing such an unusual, indeed cryptic, spelling: to keep the way to say THE NAME a secret.

In time, the Israelite priests would adopt a four-letter version of THE NAME. Why? I imagine that they did so to secure their conventional pronunciation. Adding a final letter *heh* but understanding that THE NAME was to be expressed backward, THE NAME would still function as a cryptogram. But with this change, the priests would have preserved their secret oral tradition that THE NAME was to be pronounced *Hu-Hi*, not *Hi-Hu*; "He-She," not "She-He."

We know without question that the Israelites were spelling THE NAME with four letters early in their history from archaeological findings.

On display at the Israel Museum in Jerusalem are two tiny silver amulets, each inscribed with the four-letter version of THE NAME, found during an excavation of tombs on a hill just outside Jerusalem's Old City walls in 1979. The amulets, containing a well-known passage from scripture known as the Priestly Blessing (Numbers 6:24–25), have been dated to the sixth century BCE.[49]

A pottery shard inscribed with the four-letter version of THE NAME found at Arad is as old or even older. The shard, also on display at the Israel Museum, is believed to date to the sixth or seventh century BCE.[50] Another pottery fragment inscribed with THE NAME, the Lachish Letters, discovered in 1935, also dates to this period.[51]

An even earlier artifact inscribed with the four-letter version of THE NAME is the Moabite Stone, or Mesha Stele, found in 1868 in present-day Jordan, currently on display at the Louvre Museum. The Moabite Stone has been dated to 850 BCE.[52]

Common Pronunciation

We still have to wonder how the Israelites were pronouncing THE NAME. In some biblical stories, ancient Israelites greet each other with this name. In the Book of Ruth (2:4), Boaz greets a group of harvesters, "YHWH be with you!" and the harvesters answer, "May YHWH bless you." The prophet Joel says, "Whoever will call out in the name of YHWH" will be delivered (Joel 3:5). The Psalmist declares, "I will declare Your Name to my brothers" (Psalm 22:23). According to the Mishnah (the central text around which the Talmud is organized), it had been decreed that an individual in the Temple should greet his fellow *ba'shaym* with THE NAME (Berakhot 9:5). Before the priests ruled that the personal name of God was no longer to be uttered in public, the people were pronouncing *something*; what might it have been?

Yah is a good guess for the first syllable. The syllable *yah* shows up in many theophoric names: Jeremiah in Hebrew is Yirmi*ya*; a closely related Hebrew name is Yirmi*yah*u; Isaiah in Hebrew is Yisha*yah*; and Elijah in Hebrew is Eli*yah*u. And the interjection *Hallelujah* means "You (plural) praise *Yah*!" Therefore, *Yah* was understood by the people either as a name of God or perhaps as an abbreviated name of God. (Psalm 68:5 declares that "God's name is *Yah*," while Isaiah 26:4 speaks of "*Yah* of YHWH.")[53]

As for the vocalization of the second syllable of THE NAME, WH could have sounded like *wih*, *weh*, or something similar. *Yahweh* indeed may have been how this substitute name was uttered. But the point is that *Yahweh* was a substitute name—a pseudo name—while the true pronunciation of THE NAME remained at all times a closely held, priestly secret.[54]

In regard to the switchover in spelling from the three to four letters, do we have any evidence that the tetragrammaton actually was a revised spelling of the more ancient trigrammaton? Do we have proof that the ancient Israelite priests, by adding the letter *heh*, changed the spelling of THE NAME from YHW to YHWH?

No, we do not. But we have a tantalizingly suggestive story that this indeed is what may have occurred.

In the Book of Genesis, God changes Abram's name to "Abraham" (Genesis 17:5). And then, the text tells us, God instructs Abraham to henceforth call his wife Sarai by the name "Sarah" (Genesis 17:15). In both cases the names are changed by adding the letter *heh*.⁵⁵ Hoffman notes this and believes it to be evidence of the Hebrews marking their discovery of vowel letters.

I think this parable shows more than that. By adding the letter *heh* to THE NAME of God, the priests are memorializing—albeit cryptically. The mythical story of God adding a *heh* to human names was intended to the initiated priestly elite as a reminder of a historical event in which the priests of Israel added the letter *heh* to THE NAME of God.

Having a story constructed this way, with the intention of mirroring another story, would be perfectly within the tradition of Hebrew biblical narratives. We see it all the time in the Bible. Scholars call it a typology. The story of the splitting of the Red Sea mirrors an earlier story—that of the splitting of the waters at the creation event. The story of the infant Moses riding on the water in a cradle (*tevah*) mirrors an earlier story—that of Noah riding on the water in an ark (which is the same word in Hebrew: *tevah*). The story of Laban deceiving his nephew Jacob mirrors an earlier story—that of Jacob deceiving his father, Isaac. The story of the elderly Jacob living under his son Joseph's protection in Egypt for seventeen years, so it strikes me, is meant to mirror the story of the young Joseph living under the protection of his father, Jacob, in Canaan for seventeen years.

The Hebrew Bible's story in which God adds the letter *heh* to Abram's and Sarai's names likewise mirrors an earlier story. Only in this case, it mirrors a secret story—one that was hidden to all but the priests.

CHAPTER 3

By the Rivers of Babylon: 586 BCE–70 CE

Backward writing? A secret message? A key character's name turns out to be an anagram? It all sounds more like a Harry Potter novel than the Holy Bible.

But yes, that's how the Bible reads in Hebrew. Something gets lost in translation, which is one reason why the rabbis declared the day on which the Bible was first translated (into Greek) an annual day of mourning. But once again, we are getting ahead of the story.

The Bible is not literally true in all respects, nor was it meant by its writers to be taken as literally true. Some, if not most of the stories in the Hebrew Bible are allegories, which are stories created to conceal the beliefs of an elite. The word comes from the Greek words *allos,* meaning "different," and *agoreuo,* "public speech." An allegory is therefore a different way of speaking in public.

To understand allegories, we need to look at them through a different lens, which we will do in this chapter. First, we will look at the general composition of the Hebrew Bible. Then we will take a close look at some of the stories themselves—ones that will deepen our understanding of THE NAME as a dual-gender deity, began circulating orally or in writing as early as the tenth century BCE, and reveal the Hebrew Bible to be a stunningly sophisticated literary work.

The First Temple Period

Some Jews (although far fewer than you might think) believe that the stories in the first five books of the Hebrew Bible were given by God to Moses on Mount Sinai, along with the commandments, hundreds of years earlier than the tenth century BCE. We needn't accept this to be awed by their great antiquity. The tenth century BCE is deep in the past, more than three thousand years ago. In this period Israel was shifting from a confederation of tribes led by judges to a monarchy. The First Temple in Jerusalem was built in the early years of the monarchy. And only decades after its construction, the four-letter version of THE NAME was carved into the Moabite Stone (850 BCE). So we are on solid ground when we say that the four-letter version of THE NAME was in use at the latest during the beginning of the First Temple period.

The First Temple period was a tumultuous time. After the death of the Temple's builder, King Solomon (928 BCE), the briefly united kingdom of Israel broke up. The northern kingdom took the name Israel, establishing its own monarchy and temples (I Kings 12:29). The southern kingdom, which had adopted the name Judah, maintained Jerusalem—home to Solomon's Temple and seat of the Davidic dynasty—as the center of its religious and political life.

The northern kingdom of Israel survived many wrenching upheavals until it was finally invaded by Assyria; its inhabitants—known ever after as the Ten Lost Tribes of Israel—were deported in 722 BCE. The southern kingdom of Judah, increasingly concerned about its own viability, instituted sweeping reforms. Those reforms, put in place during the reign of King Josiah (641–609 BCE), further strengthened Jerusalem's status as the cultic center. A claim was then made for which we have no earlier record: that no gods other than THE NAME were deserving of worship.

The Josiah reforms drew their authority from a book said to have been found in the Temple by the high priest Hilkiah. According to the Book of Kings, this found book was then handed over to Shaphan the Scribe, who read it to King Josiah. The female

Jerusalemite prophet Huldah was then sought out to interpret it. Finally, King Josiah read it aloud in a public ceremony in full sight of all the people gathered at Solomon's Temple in 628 BCE, renewing the covenant between the Jewish people and God.[56]

This found book is referred to as both the Book of the Teaching (Sefer ha-Torah) and the Book of the Covenant (Sefer ha-Brit).[57] We cannot be sure what this book was. Bible scholars assume this text was an early version of the Book of Deuteronomy. According to the Book of Kings, the found book forbade the worship of other gods, countryside altars, temple prostitutes, and household gods and idols. And it established (or, as the Book of Kings has it, reestablished) the observance of the festival of Passover.[58] This certainly sounds like the Book of Deuteronomy.

But in the winter of 597 BCE, a mere three decades after these sweeping reforms were promulgated, the Kingdom of Judah, like the Kingdom of Israel before it, was invaded. This time the invaders were the Babylonian army under its king Nebuchadnezzar. In the aftermath, some ten thousand people from the society's upper strata were deported to Babylonia. Judah thenceforth became a Babylonian vassal state. This state lasted only a few short years before Judah revolted and Jerusalem was besieged again. Widespread famine and untold suffering fell upon its inhabitants. Finally, in the summer of 587 BCE, the walls of the city were breached by Nebuchadnezzar's army. The Temple, and the entire city, was then utterly destroyed.[59]

The Babylonian Exile

Among the items the defeated Judean deportees were permitted to bring with them into Babylonian captivity was, presumably, the Book of the Covenant. As we will trace below, the Babylonian exile, although lasting fewer than the seventy years prophesied by Jeremiah (Jer 25:12), had a profound effect on Judean national consciousness, the written Hebrew language, and a collection of writings that in time would come to be known as the Torah ("Teaching"), otherwise known as the Five Books of Moses

(Genesis, Exodus, Leviticus, Numbers, and Deuteronomy) and to scholars as the Pentateuch.[60]

The Torah is held by Jews as especially sacred, and is read publicly in synagogues at least three days every week. (Two other sacred works, Prophets or Nevi'im and Writings or Ketuvim, complete the Hebrew Bible, which Jews refer to as the TaNaKh, an acronym for the three works Torah, Nevi'im, and Ketuvim. With its books arranged in a somewhat different order—and in the Roman Catholic and Eastern Orthodox traditions, the inclusion of some other books—Christians refer to the Hebrew Bible as the Old Testament.)

Many scholars believe that Babylonia is in all likelihood where the many stories, laws, poems, and fragments of folklore and myth which, along with the Book of the Covenant, collectively make up the Torah, were redacted (or perhaps re-redacted), woven together perhaps with some previously only oral traditions into one unified written work in the fifth century BCE. With the help of a school of scribes gathered around him, the chief redactor, many scholars believe, was likely the Israelite priest Ezra ha-Kohain the Scribe.[61]

Stories in the Hebrew Bible's Books of Ezra and Nehemiah and in the Talmud lend support to this view of Ezra. Ezra is given credit for having established the Torah after it had been forgotten by Israel and being the first person to write a Torah scroll not with old-fashioned paleo-Hebrew letters but Assyrian block script (the same script scribes use today when scribing a Torah scroll).[62]

Jewish tradition holds Ezra in such high regard that the great Talmudic sage Rabbi Yose would later go so far as to proclaim Ezra worthy of having the Torah delivered through him, had Moses not come before him.[63] Not only was Ezra both a priest and a scribe, Ezra is said to have known the secret pronunciation of THE NAME.[64] A rabbinic tradition has it that Ezra pronounced THE NAME publicly outside the Second Temple, an extraordinary, one-time-only event to mark the first public reading of the Torah in the rebuilt Jerusalem.[65] This took place around 458 BCE, about 80 years after the Jews, in an extraordinary turn of events, had been permitted to return from exile in Babylonia.)[66]

Why Ezra and his school would have embarked on the ambitious task of creating a unified Torah is not known. Some scholars believe they did this at the behest of the Persian authorities. In any event, some scholars believe that the Torah as we know it today was substantially completed by the end of the Babylonian period, when Ezra brought it to Jerusalem.

As we are about to see, the Torah treats the dual-gender secret of THE NAME delicately. If anything, Ezra and his circle of fellow scribes in Babylonia would have had even more reason to keep this ancient secret to themselves. Consider the deities their enemies worshiped: Tiglath-Pileser III, the Assyrian king who had vanquished the northern Kingdom of Israel, had worshiped a warrior god, Ashur. Nebuchadnezzar, the Babylonian king who had vanquished the southern Kingdom of Judah, had worshiped Nabu, the son of another warrior god, Marduk, who, in Babylonian mythology, had famously slain the goddess Tiamat, creating the world from her carcass. We can understand why the Jews of this time—in exile along the rivers of Babylon, praying for the full restoration of sovereignty over their land—might have wanted to avoid having a god who was in touch with his feminine side.

This was taking place during the heart of the Iron Age. Armies—Assyrian, Babylonian, and Persian—were rising up, the likes of which the world had never seen before. The social order was deeply patriarchal.[67] The gods of the Fertile Crescent's ascendant nations were all masculine, muscular, and militaristic. Had the Jewish commoners known that their priests were serving a dual-gendered god, it would not have gone over well. Other names for God found in the Hebrew Bible, such as Man O' War, seem much more in keeping with the times.[68] The Iron Age idea of a martial god would later appear in Christian and Islamic texts as well. Jesus declares "I did not come to bring peace, but a sword."[69] The Qur'an instructs Muslims to "slay the idolaters wherever you find them."[70]

For reasons old and new, the great secret, that THE NAME was a dual-gendered deity, could only be hinted at. Whether and to what extent Ezra's activities involved writing, rewriting, redacting, re-redacting, or simply scribing the Torah for the first time in Assyrian script, the deftly constructed text, which upon his return he passed to his people and to posterity—a text that would shape the course of civilization—is interlaced with hints. When read closely, it can be seen at once both revealing and concealing the great secret. In that way, it seems to have been intended for two distinct audiences at one and the same time: the initiated elite and everyone else. But if you know what to look for, the hints are everywhere.

The hints come by way of a string of stories, in which a parade of characters appear as gender fluid. Of course, you see this only when you read the Hebrew Bible in Hebrew.

Reading the Hebrew Bible in Hebrew

When the Hebrew Bible is read in translation, which is how most readers read it, all this gender fluidity gets lost. But when people read it in Hebrew, they will notice the gender fluidity almost immediately.

For example, Eve is referred to as "he." After the flood, Noah repairs to "her tent." Rebecca is referred to as a "young man." Adam is referred to as "them." Mordechai is said to have been Esther's "nursing-father." The future kings of Israel are prophesied to be "nursing kings" in the Book of Isaiah. God is addressed in both the second-person singular masculine and the second-person singular feminine. In the Book of Deuteronomy, God—"your Father"—endures the convulsions of labor, gives birth, and suckles.[71]

And the Hebrew Bible has many, many more such gender-bending instances. Even the whale in the story of Jonah appears in one verse as a male fish and in the next verse as a female fish.[72]

The gender-switching cases are not mistakes or scribal errors. They are examples of what the second-century Jerusalem scribe Ben Sira called the "twists," "obscurities," "riddles," and "hidden things" of the Torah.[73] Whatever the intentions of the biblical writers may or may not have been, as the contemporary Bible scholar James L. Kugel has observed, "the first assumption that all ancient interpreters seem to share is that the Bible is a fundamentally cryptic document."[74]

The general public was strongly discouraged from attempting to penetrate these twists, obscurities, riddles, and hidden things. "Seek not things that are too hard for you, and search not for things that are hidden from you; think upon the things that have been permitted you; you have no business with the things that are secret," Ben Sira wrote.[75] And if the people did have questions, the priests, when offering their explanations, knew how to "apply cunning," leading the people away from, not toward, the true meaning.[76]

A tradition that can be loosely translated as "What is read and what is written" helped keep the general public in the dark. The public reader of the Torah would pronounce the word for "she" when speaking of Eve, and "his tent" when speaking about Noah, notwithstanding what was written in the text. This practice of saying out loud something other than what is written in the text—called *qere* and *ketiv*—is followed to this day.[77]

While the general public was kept in the dark, discouraged from trying to fathom the text's meaning, the priests and scribes were encouraged to do just that. As the Bible scholar Karel van der Toorn has pointed out, "The protagonist of Psalm 119, held out as an example to apprentice scribes, immerses himself in the Torah *in order* to penetrate its 'mysteries' (*nipla'ot*, Psalm 119:18)."[78]

An important clue for these scribes who would penetrate the mysteries comes in another verse from the Book of Psalms. Psalm 19:13 is itself so enigmatic that it has never to my knowledge been translated literally. The Jewish Publication Society translates it as "Who can be aware of errors? Clear me of unperceived guilt." Others translate it similarly. But the most correct and profitable translation of *sh'giot mi yavin, ministarot nakeini*, would, I suggest, be the literal translation "Whosoever understands mistakes will uncover Me of My secrets."

THE NAME

A Man Named "Name" (and Other "Mistakes")

Because the Torah's great secret is that THE NAME is dual gendered, we might expect to find, in addition to mistakes relating to gender, mistakes relating to names.[79] And everywhere in the Torah, that is exactly what we find.

In the generation of the first Hebrews, Abram's and Sarai's names are changed to Abraham and Sarah; and in the second generation, Isaac's and Rebecca's names are not changed. But after that, the stories seem full of mistakes. In the third generation, Jacob's name is changed to Israel two different times, and then, in both cases, Israel's name immediately reverts back to Jacob again, after which he is referred to by both names.[80] In the fourth generation, Joseph's name is changed to Zaphenath-Paneah, but he is never once referred to by this new name.[81]

Some names are withheld at first, as if they are unknown, only to be revealed later. God tells Abram to go to an unnamed "land which I will show you," shortly revealed to be Canaan.[82] We are told that Jacob came upon a place somewhere between Beer-sheba and Haran.[83] Seven chapters later we learn the name of this place: Luz.[84] When Moses's father and mother are first introduced to us, their names seem not to be known. The text tells us only that they were "a man of the house of Levi" and "a Levite woman."[85] Four chapters later we learn that their names are in fact known: Amram and Jochebed.[86] Moses's sister is at first nameless, described only as "his sister."[87] Another twelve chapters pass by before we learn that her name is Miriam.[88] Moses's father-in-law is introduced as an unnamed "priest of Midian."[89] Then we learn that his name is Reuel.[90] A few lines later, his name has changed to Yitro (Jethro), the name by which he is called throughout the rest of the Torah (except once in the Book of Exodus, where his name is Yeter, and in the Book of Numbers, where he is once again called Reuel).[91]

Some names are withheld and never revealed. We are never told the name of Noah's wife.[92] Other than Dinah, we never learn the names of Jacob's daughters.[93] We never learn the name of the angel who changed Jacob's name to Israel.[94] We never learn the name of

Pharaoh's daughter who finds the baby Moses in the rushes, makes him her son, and, only many years later, when he is grown, bestows on him the name Moses. She is known in the Torah only as "Pharaoh's daughter."[95] So many hidden names!

Early in the story of Abraham, we are told the name of his servant, Eliezer of Damascus.[96] But when Abraham later sends his servant to find a wife for Isaac, the servant (assumed by Jewish tradition to be Eliezer) is never once referred to by name. He is repeatedly referred to simply as the "servant," then as the "man," then again as the "servant," and then as "man" and "servant." What happened to his name?[97]

Other naming oddities exist in the Bible. Jacob and Laban have, between them, three different names for the same sacred place.[98] Mount Sinai is at first called Horeb; for most of the Torah, Mount Sinai; in the Book of Deuteronomy, it is Horeb; and in the Torah's final reference, Mount Sinai.[99]

We might find it strange that parents would have different names for the same child. Yet Rachel called her and Jacob's youngest child Ben-oni, while Jacob called him Benjamin.[100] The ancestor of the Hebrew people, according to the Bible, was a man named Shem, which means "Name" (hence the term *Semites*). Who names their child Name? And then Shem appears five times listed as the first of Noah's sons (Shem, Ham, and Japeth); afterward—for no apparent reason—the names are reversed.[101]

If a character whose name is Name seems odd, consider the mountain on which Aaron dies: "Mount Mountain."[102] And the name Moses poses another dilemma. In the ancient world Moses was not a name. Moses was Egyptian for "son of"—as in Pharaoh Tuthmosis, meaning "Son of Tut." And although the text uses "Pharaoh" as if it is a proper name, it is not. Pharaoh is a title. In the Torah, we never learn the pharaoh's name. The Bible has many other such examples.[103]

We are left with a host of questions: Why in the Torah would a character's or place's name be changed more than once? Why do some name changes seem to "take" and others do not? Why does the text repeatedly hold back certain names, only to reveal them later? What meaning can be drawn from the fact that some characters are called by multiple names, or are never given a name?

The Documentary Hypothesis

According to Bible scholars of the nineteenth and twentieth centuries, the repetitions, contradictions, and discontinuities we see in the text are not that difficult to account for. They are the result of the text having been cobbled together from a variety of texts, written in different places and times and by different people who had various agendas, traditions, and versions of the same stories. The text had been poorly redacted and was further corrupted over the generations by slipshod copying.

The documentary hypothesis was enormously influential in the history of biblical scholarship. First proposed by the eighteenth-century French professor of medicine Jean Astruc and expanded on and popularized by the nineteenth-century German biblical scholar Julius Wellhausen (incorporating the work of another German scholar, Karl Heinrich Graf), the classical documentary hypothesis holds that four documents went into the making of the Pentateuch.[104] The documents are identified as J, the writer or school of writers who called God by the name YHWH (J is used because in German that is how the Hebrew letter *yod* is transliterated); E, the writer or school of writers who called God Elohim; P, the works associated with the Israelite priesthood; and D, the Deuteronomist responsible for the fifth book of the Pentateuch. By the late twentieth-century, the hypothesis had run into such difficulty that two of the supposed sources, J and E, began to be spoken of simply as "non-P" and the entire hypothesis was deemed to be in crisis.[105] But having held sway for so long, the documentary hypothesis is still considered by many as "gospel."

The J source was said to date to the tenth century BCE and the E source to the following century, followed by the D source and finally by the P source (some reverse P and D). The J source was said to be southern, the E source northern. According to the documentary hypothesis, the redactor, while arranging the final, unified text, wove these disparate texts together, which is why God is called YHWH (a southern tradition), Elohim (a northern tradition), and other names. This theory also explains why the text presents such a hodgepodge of mutually contradicting stories about the same events.

In the midtwentieth century, the Italian Bible scholar Rabbi Umberto Cassuto challenged the documentary hypothesis. But few outside of Jewish circles ever read Cassuto (or had even heard of him).[106] It was not until 1987, when R. N. Whybray, an Anglican priest and biblical scholar, made almost exactly the same argument in his book *The Making of the Pentateuch: A Methodological Study* that a new view of the authorship of the Pentateuch began to take hold.

Whybray argued that the weight of evidence no longer supported the documentary hypothesis—the idea of a redactor drawing on the works of multiple documents—but rather the idea that the Pentateuch had been the work of one author drawing on multiple sources. What led Whybray to this conclusion? The very same inconsistencies, mutually contradictory accounts, internal contradictions, and general unevenness of the text on which the documentary hypothesis rested! As Whybray put it, "The [documentary] hypothesis can only be maintained on the assumption that, while consistency was the hallmark of the various documents, inconsistency was the hallmark of the redactors."[107] The question Whybray left us with was, Why would the redactor not have smoothed all this out in the creation of the unified work?

About this Whybray did not speculate. He does not suggest why a single author, working with a variety of texts and oral traditions, would have ignored basic compositional conventions, such as internal consistency. All Whybray offered was his assessment that the overwhelming weight of evidence supported a theory of single authorship.

Robert Alter, a somewhat younger contemporary of Whybray's, noted that certain contradictions in the text appear together in such close proximity that we would be "naïve to conclude that the ancient Hebrew writer was so inept or unperceptive that the conflict between the two versions could somehow have escaped him."[108] Absent a rationale, Alter offered only that the biblical writers and redactors must have had "certain notions of unity rather different than our own," which are likely "unfathomable from the enormous distance of intellectual and historical evolution that stands between us and these creations of the early Iron Age."[109]

Alter is undoubtedly right that the text reflects a different notion of unity than our own. And yet our modern notions of unity seem to be growing increasingly more like the ancient biblical notion (more on that in chapter 7). Ironically, passing through modernity may have been a prerequisite for our being able to appreciate a central proposition embedded in this work of antiquity.

Of course, the text—like all texts and scriptures—reflects the times in which it was written. This position is not a post-Enlightenment one. The thirteenth-century Torah commentator Rabbi Abraham ibn Ezra, following the lead of second-century rabbis of the Talmud, held that the Torah could not have been a word-for-word revelation by God to Moses and at least some of the Torah had to have been written long after the times in which the stories are set.[110]

Still, by too quickly assuming that scriptural difficulties are the result of incompatible texts by multiple authors, poor redaction, and scribal errors; by smoothing over the textual rough spots in translations and commentaries and by perhaps bringing along other prejudices as well, we lose the daring sophistication and deep meaning of the work.[111]

The Medium Is the Message

Imagine that two thousand years from now, scholars came across a copy of James Joyce's novel *Ulysses*. What would they make of it? For one thing, they would be struck by the strange way the text appears on the page. The giant letters *S*, *M*, and *P* which take up almost entire pages, might be seen as an idiosyncratic printer's convention. One can imagine our forty-first-century scholars beginning their work by resetting those letters in normal-size type.

If they were lucky enough to have access to a twentieth-century *Oxford English Dictionary*, they would know that in Joyce's time "frseeeeeeeefronnnng" was not a word. They might go about emending it to "free running" (or adding the footnote "meaning of English uncertain").[112] If they had access to twentieth-century style and grammar books, our scholars of the future would understandably believe that the entire last forty-five-page section of the copy of Joyce's masterpiece that they had was corrupt, since in Joyce's time, the practice was to begin each new sentence with what was called a capital letter, and to end each sentence with a small dot known as a period. With all this information, they would produce a "corrected" text, destroying what Joyce had worked so hard to create.

What our forty-first-century scholars would have failed to grasp was that the text was not corrupt. The mistakes were not mistakes. The oversized letters, the nonsense words, and the pages upon pages of unpunctuated run-on sentences were how Joyce had intentionally written his book. He had been playing with language. The medium was the message.[113]

Such is the case with the Hebrew Bible. In important ways, we have been reading it all wrong. The Bible is exquisitely well constructed, even if its meaning is veiled, and was shaped with exceedingly deliberate intentionality, even if its message was obscured. Its primary audience, as Ben Sira tells us, was a sophisticated group of priestly scribal initiates, who were able to catch its many allusions, wordplays, coded messages, and veiled references.

Hiding in Plain Sight

Reading the opening chapter of Genesis, we see that the secret has been hiding in plain sight all along. In creating the first human being, God says "Let Us create the earth creature in Our own image." And then, the text goes on, God "created it male and female."[114] The rabbis understood this to mean that the earth creature, the *adam,* had been created by God as an intersex being, or what in earlier times was called a hermaphrodite—singular in one respect, plural in another.

Exactly how the *adam* was constituted as an intersex being was debated.

> R. Jeremiah b. Leazar said: When the Holy One, blessed be He, created Adam, He created him an hermaphrodite [bi-sexual], for it is said, *Male and female created He them and called their name Adam* (Gen v, 2.) R. Samuel b. Nahman said: When the Lord created Adam He created him doubled-faced, then He split him and made him of two backs, one back on this side and one back on the other side.[115]

The better known Adam and Eve creation story occurs in Genesis chapter 2. There, God takes a *tzayla* from the earth creature, which becomes Eve (Genesis 2:22; 3:20). The word *tzayla* is usually translated as "rib." But Rabbi Samuel bar Nachman thought otherwise. The word *tzayla*, he argues, means "side."[116] Eve was the feminine side of the androgyne earth creature, *adam*.

If we look at the entire Genesis section again we notice that Adam is not really a proper name, nor is a proper name ever conferred upon the creature. This is not a new insight. Some forty years ago, in "The Image of God in Man—Is Woman Included?" the distinguished historian of ideas Maryanne Cline Horowitz noted that the dual-gendered nature of Adam "is completely distorted by Bible translations which consistently capitalize the term as a proper name *Adam*."[117]

The first human being, the *adam* (from the word *adamah*, meaning "earth") was created male and female, or dual-gendered, in the image of God. This much the early rabbis were willing to openly say. They left it to others to make the logical inference: God, in whose image the first human being was created, is male and female.

Unity of Opposites

So what is the meaning behind all this? What is the message that the Hebrew Bible is, albeit cryptically, conveying? By presenting God—the generative force of existence—as both male and female, both singular and plural, the Hebrew Bible seems to be suggesting multiple truths: differentiated (even seemingly oppositional) forces are manifestations of an essential, fundamental unity; within that unity, reality is fluid; more than one story can, therefore, paradoxically be true; and appearances notwithstanding, the notion that reality can be divided up and placed into static, unchanging categories is an illusion. Rather, everything is one.

This philosophy has been taught in many cultures over the course of millennia. This very doctrine was taught by the mystic and philosopher Heraclitus of Ephesus (ca. 535–ca. 475 BCE), whose lifetime overlapped with the lifetime of Ezra. This concept later came to be known as the unity of opposites: nothing is static; everything flows; "one can never step into the same river twice"[118]; everything comes into being through the interplay of opposites; reality is paradoxical; and "the road is an upward-downward path."[119]

Throughout the Second Temple period—as the kingdom of Judah (with the exception of a brief period of autonomy) passed from Persian rule (589 BCE) to Greek rule (ca. 300 BCE) to Roman rule (37 BCE)—this esoteric doctrine was never taught openly by the Israelite elite, the secret of THE NAME being ever more stringently guarded.[120] As we saw in the introduction, increasingly restrictive prohibitions were imposed, outlawing the pronunciation of THE NAME by anyone but the priests.[121] Upon the death of the high priest Simon the Just (ca. 200 BCE), THE NAME was no longer uttered by the priests. The high priest pronounced it on Yom Kippur inaudibly.[122]

By the end of this period, at the time of the Second Temple's destruction in 70 CE, a millennia and a half had passed since THE NAME, in its archaic three-letter version, had been memorialized at the Temple of Soleb by Pharaoh Amenhotep's workers. That is an extremely long time for any secret to be kept. But in the history of THE NAME, an even longer period of secret keeping was about to begin.

41

CHAPTER 4

The Chain of Transmission: 70–870 CE

When the Romans destroyed the Second Temple in the year 70 CE, THE NAME was not permitted to be said aloud anywhere.

The only exception to the ban was that hereditary priests (kohanim) were permitted to teach it, on rare occasions, to other (presumably younger) hereditary priests so that the pronunciation might be passed down through the generations.

Following the destruction of the Temple, the hereditary priests felt great anxiety about the future of THE NAME. Would the secret of THE NAME survive? How exactly was this knowledge to be transmitted? Stories began circulating about folks who were old enough to have heard—or even almost heard—THE NAME pronounced. The earliest of these stories are memorialized in the great compendia of Jewish teachings from the period: the Jerusalem and Babylonian Talmuds.[123]

The traditional Jewish weekday morning prayer Supplication (*Tachanun*)—prayed to this day by observant Jews—declares, "We have not forgotten Your Name."[124] One may wonder if the chain of transmission is at all traceable. Can we identify historical figures who knew THE NAME? Do we have any evidence of how THE NAME was passed down from one generation to the next?

We can, and we do.

THE NAME speaks to us from across more than two millennia of Jewish diaspora. In this chapter we will trace the first eight hundred years of that journey, beginning with the destroyed city of Jerusalem in the year 70 CE, and then going west to the coastal city of Yavneh, north to the seat of Jewish learning in the Galilee, and finally east to the major Jewish centers of Babylonia, which brings us to the point just before the secret of THE NAME passes from Baghdad to Europe.

Late Antiquity and the Early Middle Ages, Palestine

When the Second Temple fell in the year 70 CE, the priestly elite was faced with a real predicament. On the one hand, the secret pronunciation of THE NAME could not be allowed to be lost. The hereditary priests passing THE NAME on to their successors was critical; it would need to be said aloud again by the next high priest as soon as the Temple was rebuilt.

But on the other hand, given the powers that were believed to be associated with it (which we will further trace in this chapter), equally pressing was that THE NAME not fall into the hands of people who might misuse it.

However this may seem to us, given our historical vantage point, to the priests, knowledge of THE NAME was akin to knowledge of the nuclear codes: the safety and security—indeed the very existence of their people, they believed—rested on this secret being passed to and held in the most dependable hands. The priests had been able to keep the secret of THE NAME under conditions of centralized authority in Jerusalem. But how were they to do that now, outside the confines of the Holy Precinct? In the immediate wake of the calamity, in the midst of the chaos of Jerusalem's destruction, and then over the many years yet to come, this tension between the need to both conceal and reveal would shape the Jewish relationship with THE NAME.[125]

By the year 70 CE, Rome had already demolished the Judean monarchy. The province of Iudea (as it was newly called) was now governed from Caesarea by a Roman procurator.[126] When Jerusalem fell, a second institution, the Temple cult, was for all intents and purposes abolished as well. No successor to Pinchas ben Shmuel, the last high priest, was ever named.

Only one Judean institution, the legislative and judicial body known as the Sanhedrin, was to survive intact. We owe whatever we know about the transmission of THE NAME in the years immediately following the Temple's fall to the Sanhedrin. Many of the members of the Sanhedrin were of priestly descent, although that was not a requirement of membership.[127]

Rabban Yochanan ben Zakkai, a renowned mystic, was one of the Sanhedrin's priestly members. His title—Rabban—was the honorific bestowed on Sanhedrin leaders. During the Jerusalem siege, the Sanhedrin's supreme leader Rabban Gamliel I had been killed. Rabban Yochanan ben Zakkai, his second in command, thereupon devised a plan to relocate the Sanhedrin to the coastal city of Yavneh.

In Yavneh, members of the regathered Sanhedrin would soon come to be known as rabbis. The term *rabbi* had been in use since the late Second Temple period. But only at Yavneh, after the destruction of the Temple, did it come to mean a sage.

The earliest stories we have about the transmission of THE NAME after the fall of the Second Temple come to us from these rabbis. In one of the stories, Rabbi Tarfon (active 80–110 CE), a priestly member of the Yavneh Sanhedrin, recounts how in Jerusalem he had stood in line with the priests as they were reciting the priestly blessing, turned his ear toward the high priest; and how he heard the high priest murmur THE NAME under the melody of the priests.[128]

The Sanhedrin had to relocate again, this time from Yavneh to the Galilee, in the wake of a disastrous Jewish Messianic uprising in the second century called the Bar Kokhba Revolt (133 CE). There, the rabbis of the Galilean Sanhedrin shared miracle stories ascribing supernatural power to THE NAME. The Sanhedrin's supreme leader of the late second century, the quasi-monarchal Judah ha-Nasi (active 170–200 CE), claimed that King David (from whom he claimed descent) had been saved in battle thanks to THE NAME. According to the story, King David's nephew Abishai pronounced THE NAME, whereupon the king was momentarily levitated above the battleground. When the danger passed, Abishai pronounced THE NAME again, and David was safely returned to earth.[129]

Another genre of stories from the rabbis of the Galilean Sanhedrin memorialized attempts by various people to learn the secret of THE NAME. In one such story, Rabbi Inyani bar Susai (active 220–250 CE) seemed prepared to reveal the secret of THE NAME to Rabbi Chanina, whom he was visiting in Tzippori. But when Rabbi Chanina's son was found hiding under the bed eavesdropping (an ill-timed sneeze had given the boy away), Inyani bar Susai refused to reveal THE NAME to either of them.[130] Another story tells how Rabbi Pinchas bar Chama (active 220–250 CE) declined to learn THE NAME from a certain doctor in Tzippori, who was ready to divulge it, because Rabbi Pinchas partook of tithes, and one who was familiar with THE NAME was not permitted to derive benefit from others.[131] In yet another story that illustrates the trouble the dispersed priestly class had with keeping the secret, a man was said to have uttered THE NAME in the act of cursing his son. The son died, and the man was filled with a two-fold sorrow: for the loss of his son, and also for THE NAME having been unintentionally revealed to a man named Shmuel, who heard it pronounced as he was passing by at the time.[132]

Rome recognized the Sanhedrin's supreme leader as the leader of the Jewish people and accorded this leader the title "patriarch." The office of the patriarch was not formally abolished by Rome until around 425 CE. However, by the mid- to late third century, during a period in which famine and lawlessness were ravaging the Roman Empire, the center of Jewish life had decisively shifted away to Babylonia.

Late Antiquity and Early Middle Ages, Babylonia

In Babylonia, Jews held more interest in magic, demons, and the occult than they had in Israel. In Babylonia, miracle tales about the power of THE NAME grew increasingly popular and began to involve living sages. The Babylonian Talmud claims that Rabbis Chanina and Oshaya used a coded instruction manual called the Book of Formation (Sefer Yetzirah)—and, according to Rashi (Rabbi Shlomo Yitzhaki, 1040–1105 CE), secret knowledge of THE NAME—to perform a weekly miracle.[133] According to the Talmudic story, each Friday afternoon, Rabbis Chanina and Oshaya would create a calf, just before the onset of the Sabbath.[134] The Book of Formation passed among Jewish mystics, albeit in a variety of edited versions, or recensions, from as early as the third century.

In time, the Babylonian Jewish community's formal institutions came to mirror those of Palestine. As in Palestine, academies of learning were established, the most prominent of which were in the cities of Sura and Nehardea (and then Nehardea's successor, Pumbedita). Each academy had a Sanhedrin, in time headed by an excellency (*gaon*, akin to *nasi*, the Palestinian term "prince") and chief justice (*av bet din*).[135] And just as the Romans, in what came to be called Syria-Palaestina (Palestine), recognized a patriarch as the leader of the Jewish community in exile, the Persian (and later Arab) rulers of Babylonia recognized an exilarch (*Resh Galuta*).[136]

The Babylonian Jews were a proud people. They held their lineage to be as old as, if not older than, the lineage of the Palestinian Jews. The exilarch claimed to be descended from King Jehoiachin, who had been exiled to Babylonia after the fall of the First Temple. Jehoiachin's lineage, in turn, was said to have dated all the way back to King David. A prayer of petition for the Davidic Messiah, recited to this day, was initially added to the Standing Prayer (*Amidah*) in Babylonia "out of esteem for the dynasty of the Exilarch."[137]

The many mystical traditions of the Babylonian Jews—so the Babylonian Jews of late antiquity and the Middle Ages believed—had originated with the late sixth-century BCE prophet Ezekiel. Ezekiel, a member of the priestly class and therefore intimate with knowledge of the Jerusalem Temple and its workings, had been among the Jewish aristocrats exiled to Babylonia in 597 BCE. The Babylonian Talmud connects certain mystical traditions having to do with THE NAME to Ezekiel. But although noted, they are never explained. According to Rabbi Chiyya (active 200–220 CE), the secrets were so closely guarded that a teacher was permitted to teach his student only the chapter headings.[138]

In the Talmud, the mystical school based on the Book of Ezekiel is referred to as Workings of the Chariot (*Ma'aseh Merkabah*). Another early school of Jewish mysticism existed as well, called Workings of Creation (*Ma'aseh Bereishit*). According to these schools, if one knew THE NAME, one could unlock secrets somehow hidden in the opening chapter of the Book of Genesis and the Book of Ezekiel. According to Chariot mysticism, an adept could use knowledge of THE NAME to rise to higher and higher spiritual planes, ultimately to the highest level, into the very presence of God. The doctrine was selectively taught. The Mishnah (codified ca. 200 CE), uses terms like *Concealments of the Torah* (*Sitrei Torah*) or *Secrets of the Torah* (*Razei Torah*) when referring to this doctrine, and it makes clear that teaching this doctrine to more than one worthy student at a time is prohibited.[139]

Stories about mystical adepts who were said to have possessed knowledge of THE NAME are sprinkled throughout both the Babylonian and Jerusalem Talmuds.[140] These references are all couched in exceedingly elliptical language. But the early mystical masters hint that the Books of Genesis and Ezekiel, when properly understood, reveal the secret that God is, so to speak, dual gendered, and if the letters of THE NAME are properly reordered, the truth is revealed.

The Book of Ezekiel, if read in English, in no way seems to hint at the dual-gender secret of THE NAME. But reading Ezekiel in Hebrew is another matter altogether. In Hebrew, one immediately notices a persistent conflation of grammatical gender, persistent, and overwhelming. Everywhere one looks in Ezekiel, masculine nouns are modified by feminine adjectives and feminine nouns are modified by masculine adjectives. The phenomenon is so pervasive in Hebrew that a prominent mid twentieth-century Bible scholar went so far as to suggest that the prophet Ezekiel must have suffered from "gender confusion."[141] Some Muslims believe Ezekiel to be the mysterious figure Dhul-Kifl, who appears in Sura 21 and Sura 38 of the Qur'an, and is described as a righteous man and counted among Islam's prophets. The name Dhul-Kifl means "the Double One."

As to the meaning of all this, the rabbis were silent. They would go so far as to direct their curious students' attention to only the last line of the Book of Ezekiel. Rabbi Shmuel b. Nachmani (active 290–320 CE) taught, in the name of Rabbi Yochanan, that the last line of the Book of Ezekiel (48:35) should not be vocalized as YHWH *shamah*, "THE NAME is there." The Babylonian Talmud says, "Do not read 'there' (*shamah*). Rather read 'Her Name' (*shemah*)."[142]

That was a pretty good hint. Other hints, according to the rabbis, had been left in other books of the Hebrew Bible. The rabbis pointed to a passage in the Book of Daniel, in which God is described as both sitting on a "throne" (singular) and sitting on "thrones" (plural), suggesting, to the mystically inclined, a deity who is at once both singular and plural.[143] Later mystics would point to a line in the Song of Songs, where the "king" (singular) dwells in "chambers" (plural).[144]

A prominent Babylonian Jewish mystic was Rava (active 320–350 CE), head of the Pumbedita academy. Rava is our source for another miracle tale regarding THE NAME. According to Rava, the prophet Isaiah (eighth century BCE) uttered THE NAME and was thereupon swallowed by a cedar tree.[145] Rava himself, so the Babylonian Talmud claims, knew THE NAME and used it to create a human being, which he sent to his friend Rav Zera.[146]

Such magical use of THE NAME would, in time, be considered scandalous. But in the Babylonia of late antiquity and early Middle Ages, magic was accepted. In Babylonia, a new professional class of Jewish healers and wonder-workers arose who were said to know how to use THE NAME to ward off evil spirits. These shamanic healers and wonder-workers would come to be known as the Masters of THE NAME (*Ba'alei Shem*). If the testimony of the late second-century to early third-century Christian theologian Origen is accurate, these Masters of THE NAME were sought out by not only Jews but possibly non-Jews as well. Archaeological evidence seems to support this. So-called incantation bowls (thought to have the power to ward off demons) were produced by shamanic Jews for the benefit of clients who had what seem to be Persian and Christian names.¹⁴⁷ This shamanic knowledge was a closely held secret.

The holy "names treated with so much reverence among the Hebrews," Origen writes, were among those names—Egyptian and Persian included—"known to exceedingly few . . . [which] belong to a secret theology which refers to the Framer of all things . . . efficacious against certain demons . . . [and which] when pronounced with that attendant train of circumstances which is appropriate to their nature, are possessed of great power."¹⁴⁸

But to produce the effect, one had to know how to pronounce THE NAME in its original language. THE NAME would not work if translated into Greek or Arabic. According to Origen, "If we translate . . . we shall accomplish nothing; whereas if we retain the original pronunciation, we shall, as those who are skilled in such matters maintain, produce some effect."¹⁴⁹

The Masters of THE NAME would ward off evil spirits by creating amulets and by saying incantations that employed the letters of THE NAME. How new was this use of THE NAME? Had THE NAME been used this way by any Jews before the fall of the Second Temple? These questions are hard to answer. Evil spirits and demons go almost unmentioned in the Torah.¹⁵⁰ We do not see them mentioned to any great extent in the Jerusalem Talmud. In contrast, demons are ubiquitous in the Babylonian Talmud, the implication being that demon obsession was a later, Babylonian-influenced affair.¹⁵¹ Whatever the circumstances and forces were that had resulted in the rise of this Jewish shamanic class, by the late ninth century, eight hundred years after the destruction of Jerusalem, the Masters of THE NAME had carved out a role for themselves in Jewish society that helped ensure the continued passage of THE NAME for generations to come.

CHAPTER 5

The Wandering Secret: 870–1492 CE

B y the ninth century, the center of gravity in the Jewish world was shifting again, this time from Babylonia to Europe. The traditions and even languages of the long-dispersed Jews had, by the ninth century, grown increasingly globally diverse. In Europe alone, Sephardi Jews populated Spain and Portugal; Ashkenazi Jews centered in northern Europe's Rhineland; Romaniote Jews had established communities in Greece; and Italkim Jews made their home in Italy. To the east, the Malabari, or Cochin, Jews lived in India, some of whom continued farther eastward to found the Chinese Jewish Tiao Jin Jiao community; to the south, Beta Yisrael Jews resided in African Ethiopia; and Mizrachi, or "Eastern," Jews stretched across Babylonia, Yemen, the greater Arabian Peninsula, North Africa, and Israel. The Jews were a far-flung people.

Italy was the lynchpin between the old Jewish center back in Babylonia and the newly populous Jewish communities of Europe. Roman Jews had roots going back as far as 161 BCE, when the Hasmonean Jewish leader Judah Maccabee had first sent ambassadors there.[152] The secret of THE NAME might have been known to some descendants of those early Jewish emigrants to Rome.

But according to Jewish tradition, the full esoteric tradition of THE NAME, which had been preserved in Babylonia for close to a millennium, arrived in Italy in the midninth century. These traditions were brought to Italy from Babylonia by a mysterious figure by the name of Aaron of Baghdad (otherwise known as Abu Aaron). Settling in southern Italy, he was known to the Jews as "Father of All the Secrets" (*Av Kol ha-Sodot*), European Jewry's link to its esoteric past. Little is known about him, but he was considered to have exceeded all the other Masters of THE NAME.

In or around the year 870, Aaron of Baghdad tutored a northern Italian rabbi called Moses ben Kalonymus of Lucca in the secrets of THE NAME. Thereafter, when Rabbi Moses relocated to Germany, he established a mystical school based on those ancient secrets. The Kalonymuses of Lucca were a very prominent family. They had been, so one story goes, personally invited to settle in Mainz, Germany by Charlemagne in 787. Aaron of Baghdad thus had passed his secrets on to not just anyone, but to a member of a family equivalent in the Jewish world to European royalty.

The Jewish mystical tradition did not disappear from Italy after the removal of Rabbi Moses to Germany. It continued under such Masters of THE NAME as Shephatiah Ba'al Shem of southern Italy, a liturgical poet; and his son Amittai Ba'al Shem. But in Germany the famous and prominent family of Kalonymus rabbis would preserve, transmit, and explicate THE NAME for a thousand years. Kalonymus (a name that dates back to Talmudic times) is Greek for "beautiful name."

Was the spreading knowledge of THE NAME a good thing? It depends on whom you asked. The increasing dissemination of Judaism's esoteric knowledge was of course inevitable. For instance, the "instruction manual" the Book of Formation (*Sefer Yetzirah*) could not be taken out of circulation once it had been disseminated throughout the Jewish world. Even the eminent tenth-century Rav Saadiah Gaon of Babylonia, which was still the center of the Jewish world at the time, had written a commentary on it. Yes, the Book of Formation was written in highly veiled language, presumably understandable only to the Masters of THE NAME. But it seems clear, at least from the version that has come down to us, that this book was giving instruction on the manipulation of the letters of THE NAME.

In the ancient world, Jewish mystics had practiced a form of meditation that involved sitting for long periods of time with their heads between their knees (the practice was said to go back to the ninth-century BCE prophet Elijah, according to I Kings 18:42). But by the Middle Ages, the stories circulating about the Masters of THE NAME had grown increasingly fantastic, and people regarded them for more than their ability to sit still for long periods of time.

By the eleventh century, a claim was being made that back in Babylonia, the Masters of THE NAME had gone beyond creating animals and human beings. According to Rav Hai Gaon, who was the head of the Babylonian Talmudic academy in eleventh-century Pumbedita, the Masters of THE NAME were said to have mastered control of time and space. Witnesses had "testified that they had seen a certain man, one of the well-known *Ba'alei Shem*, on the eve of the Sabbath in one place, and that at the same time he was seen in another place, several days' journey distant."[153] It bears noting how much this story of instantaneous travel sounds like stories told earlier by and about Sufi Muslim saints, such as Ibrahim ibn Adham (ca. 718–ca. 782). One senses a sort of shamanic can-you-top-this competition ("My people's holy men are more powerful than your people's holy men").

In any event, stories such as these made the Masters of THE NAME scandalous in the eyes of the rabbis, who at the time were concerned with issues of Jewish law, pedagogy, and communal welfare. The Masters of THE NAME operated in a different orbit; paid for by private clients, they were solo practitioners, if you will. This system was acceptable in Babylonia since the culture was different there. But in Europe—in the New World—they were an embarrassment. It was one thing for the Masters of THE NAME to preserve and pass on the secret for the sake of future priests, contemplate THE NAME in private meditation, even engage in small-circle philosophical speculation about THE NAME. It was quite another thing for the Masters of THE NAME to presume to use THE NAME for magical (albeit "good") purposes.

When people in Europe heard that the Masters of THE NAME had reportedly been using THE NAME to facilitate the instantaneous collapse of great distances and other feats of magic, the reaction was immediately and unreservedly critical. The Spanish Jewish poet-philosopher Rabbi Yehuda (Judah) Halevi (1075–1141) railed against the Masters of THE NAME. In his book the

Kuzari, Halevi declares that they could not have done all that just by uttering the same words that a prophet had once uttered.[154] Perhaps they knew THE NAME—Halevi was not saying they did not. But, he wrote, one should not believe that when miracles had been performed for the prophets, "words alone were the reason for the miracle."[155]

With Halevi we can see the historical balance tipping away from concern that THE NAME might be lost and back toward concern that THE NAME might be misused. But the issue was far from settled. And a new work was about to reveal more than had ever been revealed about the long-held secret of THE NAME.

The Beginning of Kabbalah

By the end of the twelfth century, a new school of Jewish mysticism was beginning to emerge in Europe. Known as Kabbalah (the "Received" tradition), this school was founded around 1180, around the time a new work appeared in Provence, France. This work, a landmark in the history of THE NAME, circulated at first only in manuscript form among a very small circle. It was the first to shed light on the dual-gender secret of THE NAME. The book was called, appropriately, the Book of Bright Light (Sefer ha-Bahir).

Bright light—any light—would have been welcomed by the Jews of Europe's dark twelfth century. Europe was still in a state of chaos, as it had been ever since the collapse of the Roman Empire seven hundred years earlier. The Roman Senate had been returned to a cow pasture; Rome's population of one million was down to a mere forty thousand souls. Goths, Huns, Vandals, and other tribes swept back and forth across the continent. Monastic libraries across Italy, France, and Bavaria were being torched, frightening everyone and deeply depressing the few who could actually read. Personal disputes of the era were settled by duel or ordeal. A standard feature of the European legal systems of the time (we might not recognize them as legal systems today) was torture. Punishment was barbaric.[156] Personal hygiene was unknown. Sewage and offal ran freely in open gutters. Epidemics erupted and raged out of control.

Superstition stood in the place of science. And demons were everywhere, wreaking every imaginable sort of havoc, or were at least capable of doing so at any moment, or so it was believed.

And the Jews of medieval Europe had their own special miseries. In 1066, Muslims had massacred the Jews of Granada, Spain; an event unprecedented since the Moorish invasion of the Iberian Peninsula in 711. Thirty years later, in 1096, Christian Crusaders had massacred the Jews of Rouen, France, and then careened down Germany's Rhineland, torturing and slaughtering the Jews of Speyer, Worms, Mainz, and Cologne. (The Jewish tradition of reciting a memorial prayer—formally known as the Sanctification [prayer] of Orphans, or *Kaddish Yatom*—began as a way for the untold number of Jewish orphans of Germany to publicly mourn their parents.) Fifty years later, fanatical Almohad Muslims had forced conversion on the Jews in Andalusia, Spain.[157] A few decades after that, France experienced its first blood libel, the false accusation that Jews murder Christian children in their religious rituals: thirty-one Jewish men, women, and children were burned at the stake by their Christian neighbors.

The Book of Bright Light begins therefore fittingly with a line taken from the Book of Job: "And now they do not see light, which is brilliant (*bahir*) in the skies." God who created the world from "chaos and desolation" is hidden behind "cloud and dark."[158] Petrarch, one of the fathers of the Renaissance, would use those very words when he looked back and gave a name to Europe's medieval era, calling it the Dark Ages.[159]

And yet the Book of Bright Light tells its readers one must never forget that God is still here, hidden within the darkness. The key is not to fear—or rather, the key is to fear only God. Yes, evil is real, but the darkness in which God is hiding is not. Maintain a calm voice, accept your suffering with love, and know that evil can be overcome in study, because when one studies the Torah for its own sake, one marries the male and female aspects of God—the "Bride" and "Blessed Holy One"—together. To study the Torah is to be complete with God and at peace and know the truth. And the truth is that balance will one day be restored to the world because the heart of heaven is male and female.

Powerless in the material world, the Jewish mystics sought to transcend it. The Book of Bright Light was their guide—a text still cautious but more revelatory than any previous text and much more forthcoming than the earlier, more tersely worded Book of Formation. That God has, so to speak, male and female aspects was something that had never been openly acknowledged before. This was something new. Perhaps the mystics justified their decision to reveal this because it served to further differentiate them from their Christian persecutors who, it was known, prayed to a male God (the church's teaching at the time was emphatic that only men—not women—had been created in God's image).[160]

Also new was the Book of Bright Light's description of a series of divine, dynamic "emanations" (*sefirot*, first encountered in the Book of Formation), or a chain of increasingly present aspects of God. Later Kabbalists would give names to all the emanations, but the Book of Bright Light names only one: the Shekhinah. The term had been heard before. In the Talmud, *shekhinah* means God's "presence," the aspect of God immediately available to human beings, interacting with them. But, though grammatically feminine, the word as used in the Talmud did not, at least openly, designate a divine feminine aspect or power. In the Book of Bright Light, it means exactly that.[161] Not long after the appearance of the Book of Bright Light, the idea that God was dual gendered would be widely accepted in the Jewish world. Within a hundred years, with the publication of the Zohar (to which we will shortly turn), it would be utterly normative.[162]

So what exactly does the Book of Bright Light reveal about THE NAME? That's hard to say. Structurally, this work is written in the style of a handbook of frequently asked questions. And yet the answers that the Book of Bright Light provides are still highly guarded. For example, it says "The [four letters of THE NAME] *Yod Heh Vav Heh* can be permuted 24 different ways."[163] But what exactly are we meant to do with that information?

What the Book of Bright Light indicates is that we are looking at the letters of THE NAME in the wrong order. The letters of THE NAME need to be rearranged, the Book of Bright Light tells us, and—most importantly—we are *permitted* do this. Despite what we may have heard to the contrary, Rabbi Ahilai, one of the sages who is quoted in the book, claims that a verse in the Torah makes it clear, regarding THE NAME, that "permission was given that it be permuted and spoken." The reference is to Numbers 6:27, which reads, "And they shall place My name upon the children of Israel, and I will bless them."

Over and over again the Book of Bright Light returns to the theme of dual gender. We are told outright that "the Blessed Holy One created Adam *male and female*." The biblical character Tamar had been singled out, we are told, "because she included both male and female." We are told that certain letters of the Hebrew alphabet somehow "include male and female." Regarding the Torah's two different versions of the Ten Commandments, the Book of Bright Light asks why one version says to "remember the Sabbath" (Exodus 20:8) while the other version says to "keep the Sabbath" (Deuteronomy 5:12). The Book of Bright Light's answer is this: "Remember [*zachor*] refers to the male [*zachar*]; keep [*shamor*] refers to the bride." The idea of a "sacred marriage" between God's male and female aspects appears for the first time in the Book of Bright Light. Regarding the scribal tradition of beginning a Torah scroll with an oversized letter *bet*, the Book of Bright Light tells us that the letter *bet* (which can also be read as the number two) represents the union of masculine and feminine, united in the primordial act of Creation. Speculating on the Messianic age, the Book of Bright Light tells us that the time of the Messiah is to be the moment of the reunion of masculine and feminine.

A new (or perhaps newly revealed) reason behind the ancient Temple's Holy of Holies is presented. The Book of Bright Light asks, and then answers, "What is the meaning of Holy of Holies? It means that it is holy for the Holy Ones [meaning the male and female aspects of God]." God, according to the Book of Bright Light, is the perfect unity of male and female; and we must do our duty "to recognize and know the Unity of Unities, who is unified in all His names." Earthly males and females are simply reflections of the male and female aspects of God: "The soul of the female comes from the Female [aspect of God], and the soul of the male comes from the Male [aspect of God]."[164]

Opposition to Kabbalah

Ten years after the appearance of this first work of Kabbalah, the Book of Bright Light, the great Jewish philosopher Maimonides (Rabbi Moses ben Maimon, 1135–1204) published his Guide for the Perplexed (1190). Maimonides was born in Córdoba, Spain, but fled with his family following the fall of the city in 1148 to the Almohads, ultimately resettling in Cairo, Egypt.

Maimonides is revered as one of Judaism's greatest rabbis. But he was also one of its most controversial. Maimonides was a rationalist who lent credence to such non-Jewish Aristotelian ideas as the eternity of the world.[165] But rationalist though he was, Maimonides, in the Guide for the Perplexed, presents his reader with a treatise on the two great ancient schools of Jewish mysticism: the Workings of Creation and Workings of the Chariot. Maimonides was not a Kabbalist. He strongly disagreed with the newly emerging Kabbalistic idea of divine emanations. He found it an offense to God's absolute unity.[166]

But no less than the Kabbalists, Maimonides understood the early mystical Workings of Creation and Workings of the Chariot as containing keys to unlocking secrets hidden in the books of the prophets and the Torah. And of all the secrets these works were said to unlock, according to Maimonides, no secret was greater than the secret of THE NAME. All the other names for God in the Hebrew Bible were derived names—indeed, merely descriptions.[167] THE NAME alone is the only name indicative of God's true essence.[168] People would be mistaken, Maimonides taught, if they believed that the sages who transmitted THE NAME to their disciples had taught them only the pronunciation of the letters. What was being passed on as well was the meaning of THE NAME "because of which the

Tetragrammaton was made a *nomen proprium* [proper name] of God, and which includes certain metaphysical principles."[169]

And what is the meaning of THE NAME? What is the metaphysical principle included within the *nomen proprium* of God? Maimonides believed he had hit upon it. No teacher, he tells us, had explained it to him nor had he received it through any sort of divine revelation. He had come to his understanding "based on reasoning."[170] And if the reader will now but follow him closely, he will "obtain a perfect and clear insight into all that has been clear and intelligible to me. This is the utmost that can be done in treating this subject so as to be useful to all without fully explaining it."[171]

Maimonides is prepared to divulge the explanation that "was never committed to writing."[172] The only problem is he cannot divulge it openly. Maimonides will not be "a revealer of secrets."[173] After all, limits have been placed on what may be "divulged to the multitude."[174] Such limits serve a good purpose, because if the secret of THE NAME were spoken publicly, people might misunderstand and take it to mean that God "consists of two elements."[175]

And so Maimonides must speak circumspectly. At one point, he writes, "To give a full explanation of the mystic passages of the Bible is contrary to the Law and to reason."[176] And cryptically he adds, "In some instances it will be sufficient if you understand from my remarks that a certain expression contains a figure, although I may offer no other comment. For when you know that it is not to be taken literally, you will understand at once to what subject it refers."[177]

Maimonides informs his reader that throughout his work, clues have been "scattered, and are interspersed with other topics," his purpose in adopting such an arrangement being that "the truths should be at one time apparent, and at another time concealed."[178] He cautions his reader to be on the lookout. Glimpses of understanding are likely to come as "flashes of lightning" that appear and then just as quickly disappear.[179] The clues, once discerned as such, will have to be strung together by the reader, as a "clever man joined cord with cord, and rope with rope, and drew up and drank" otherwise inaccessible water from a well.[180] The reader is advised to "attend to every term mentioned therein, although it may seem to have no connection with the principal subject. . . . Nothing of what is mentioned is out of place."[181]

With all these caveats and prompts in place, Maimonides, in chapter 63 of the Guide for the Perplexed, expounds on a name of God—not THE NAME but what Maimonides calls one of the derivative names: "I am that I am," *Ehyeh Asher Ehyeh*. Maimonides cannot teach on THE NAME directly, so this will have to do. And here is what he has to say:

> The principal point in this phrase is that the same word which denotes existence, is repeated as an attribute. The word *asher*, "that," corresponds to the Arabic *illadi* and *illati*, [*alladhi* and *allati*, the male and female relative pronouns] and is an incomplete noun that must be completed by another noun; it may be considered as the subject of the predicate which follows.[182]

Why is Maimonides drawing attention to both the male and female relative pronouns in Arabic? This seems out of place, given that God is understood to be masculine. But keep in mind that Maimonides has elsewhere put the reader on notice that "nothing of what is mentioned is out of place." Moreover, Maimonides has declared that those who read his interpretation "will believe that I have . . . only, as it were, translated from one language into another."[183]

Maimonides cannot teach the secret of THE NAME directly. He has told us so. What he is doing by expounding on the so-called derivative name "I am that I am" is teaching by analogy. Just as "I am that I am" is, in Hebrew, a palindrome (*Ehyeh Asher Ehyeh*), read forward and backward, so too must THE NAME be read forward and backward. Just as *Ehyeh Asher Ehyeh* was revealed to Moses but only *Ehyeh* was revealed through Moses to the Israelites (Exodus 3:14), so, too, THE NAME was not and cannot be revealed to the everyday Israelite.[184] Just as the word *asher* ("that") is expressed by the male and female relative pronouns in Arabic, so does THE NAME reveal itself when one considers the male and female personal pronouns in Hebrew.

Finally, Maimonides notes, God will draw a prophet's attention to an object and then to a second object, "the name of which has neither etymologically nor homonymously any relation to the first object, but *the names of both contain the same letters, though in a different order* [my italics]. In this way we find very strange things and also mysteries."[185]

But is not the idea of God's dual gender, according to Maimonides, an offense to the absolute unity of God? Once again, Maimonides instructs by analogy. Adam and Eve, created in God's image, "were two in some respects, and yet they remained one."[186] Then he offers obliquely, "How great is the ignorance of those who do not see that all this necessarily includes some [other] idea [besides the literal meaning of the words]."[187]

The "idea" that Maimonides refers to, it should be clear by now, is God's so-to-speak dual gender. But, again, this is not to be taken literally. Linguistically, THE NAME is composed of approximations of the male and female pronouns in Hebrew. But Maimonides, ever concerned that this idea not be misconstrued, takes pains to point out that "languages are conventional . . . not natural."[188] God, Maimonides wants to be sure his reader understands, is beyond gender. God is pure being and existent in a way that no other being is, and God's binity, or more accurately dual-within-unitive existence, is hinted at "by means of similes taken from physical bodies."[189]

Early Thirteenth Century, Germany

In thirteenth-century Germany, the German Pietists (*Hasidei Ashkenaz*)—under the leadership of Rabbi Judah ben Samuel of Regensburg, scion of the illustrious Kalonymus family—were of the opinion that the fewer hints the better. Rabbi Judah (also known as Yehudah he-Hasid, or Judah the Pious, 1150–1217) was heir to the treasure trove of secrets said to have been passed down from Aaron of Baghdad. As leader of the circle of German Pietists, Rabbi Judah was the chief proponent of an esoteric and mystical theology; he was a religious elitist whose personal religious practice was austere, hardly a path for everyone. A miracle worker, so legend says, he had a reputation as a man of exacting temperament. The devotional circle he led was, by intention, incredibly small. He admitted no one to that circle who was not utterly committed to his vision of pietistic perfection. He wrote down some teachings, yes, but in line with what earlier sages had held, he believed the deepest secrets should be passed on only from mouth to ear, from one pious teacher to one proven, eminently worthy student at a time. He was frustrated by the fact that the Book of Bright Light had been published and could not be unpublished. Events were overtaking Rabbi Judah's wish to maintain his single-handedly strict control over the corpus of yet unrevealed Jewish esoteric knowledge.

When Rabbi Judah died in 1217, his trusted student Rabbi Eleazar ben Judah of Worms (ca. 1165–ca. 1230) made a fateful decision. Everything Rabbi Judah had known about THE NAME had been passed to Rabbi Eleazar, his fellow Kalonymus family member. During Rabbi Judah's lifetime, Rabbi Eleazar was diligent about keeping the old man's secrets. But when Rabbi Judah died, Rabbi Eleazar sat down and began writing his Book of Wisdom (Sefer ha-Chokhmah), revealing many of the heretofore unrevealed secrets. Why would he do such a thing?

In the introduction to this work, Rabbi Eleazar cited personal calamities as his reasons for revealing secrets that had never before been shared in writing. Chief among them, in 1196, his wife Doulcea and daughters Hannah and Bellete had been slaughtered during a Crusader attack on the family's home and Rabbi Eleazar and his son had in the course of the assault been badly wounded.

In the introduction to his Book of THE NAME (Sefer HaShem), the first work to deal extensively with the secret of THE NAME, Rabbi Eleazar described in detail, and for the first time in writing, what we presume to have been up until that time an oral tradition passed down through the generations of the Kalonymus family.[190] He included a description of THE NAME being transmitted from master to disciple:

> The name is transmitted only to the reserved—this word can also be translated as 'the initiate'—who are not prone

to anger; who are humble and God-fearing, and carry out the commandments of their Creator. And it is transmitted only over water. Before the master teaches it to his pupil, they must both immerse themselves and bathe in forty measures of flowing water, then put on white garments and fast on the day of instruction. Then both must stand up to their ankles in the water, and the master must say a prayer ending with the words: 'The voice of God is over the waters! Praised be Thou, O Lord, who revealest Thy secret to those who fear Thee, He who knoweth the mysteries.' Then both must turn their eyes to the water and recite verses from the Psalms, praising God over the waters.[191]

But more than just the transmission ritual was being revealed. In his work, Rabbi Eleazar introduced the term the Secret of [God's] Unity (*Sod ha Yichud*), another part of the legacy that had been passed to him from Rabbi Judah the Pious. As the Jews have always said, quoting the Torah, "God is One," but what does that mean? According to Rabbi Eleazar, Rabbi Judah had taught him to see wine-soaked bread as an analogy for God's unity: the wine is completely swallowed up by the bread and the bread is completely saturated by the wine. Rabbi Judah, a mystic, was expressing what Maimonides, a rationalist philosopher, said in different words: God is two in a certain respect but essentially and inextricably one. Wine is not bread, and bread is not wine. But in wine-soaked bread, the elements cannot be individuated. Such, Rabbi Eleazar taught in the name of his teacher, is God's all-pervasive unity.

Early Thirteenth Century, Provence

Like the Spanish-born anti-Kabbalist Maimonides, Rabbi Eleazar ben Judah, the last of the Jewish-German pre-Kabbalah mystics, struggled to reveal without revealing too much. Nowhere in either of their writings is it explicitly stated that THE NAME signifies God as male and female. But that was about to change. The Kabbalists, despite their reputation for secretiveness, would, in fits and starts, ultimately end up revealing so much about THE NAME that in time, in the Jewish world, the dual gender, reverse spelling, pronunciation, and meaning of THE NAME would be all but an open secret.

The Kabbalist Isaac the Blind of Provence (ca. 1160–1235), who was about twenty years old when the anonymous Kabbalistic work the Book of Bright Light appeared, is the first Kabbalist known to us by name to have set down any of his teachings in writing and the first Jewish mystic known to have devoted the entirety of his work to Kabbalah. (His father, the Talmudist and prolific writer Abraham ben David of Posquieres known as Rabad, is said to have passed certain mystical teachings on to his son, but as far as we know he committed none of those teachings to writing.)

Kabbalah offered the Jews hope. In the darkness of the early thirteenth century, Kabbalah taught that they could take comfort in the simple observance of nature. Every aspect of nature, Isaac the Blind taught, reflects God's masculine and feminine potencies. For instance, when Genesis 1:5 says, "God called the light day," according to Isaac the Blind, "day" signifies God's masculine aspect, while "night" signifies God's feminine aspect. And yet, the masculine and feminine powers are one, an insight he inferred from the next line, "And there was evening and there was morning, one day."[192]

In his explication of the opening verses of Genesis, from which the above is derived, Isaac the Blind declares "The end is feminine."[193] The simple reference here is to the dry land of Genesis (the word in Hebrew, *yabashah*, is grammatically feminine).[194] But "the end is feminine" is also a reference to Israel and to the end, or last of the divine emanations (*sefirot*), which is known as the Shekhinah—the grammatically feminine term meaning "presence," now openly spoken of as God's feminine aspect. Isaac the Blind's declaration "the end is feminine" can also be read as a hint: when the letters of the tetragrammaton are arrayed in their proper (i.e., reverse) order, "the end" of THE NAME is the feminine pronoun *hi* ("she").

To Isaac the Blind, and the growing circle of Kabbalists, wordplay—a hallmark of the Torah—was a way of understanding God. All language, with its male and female grammatical forms, is at its root connected to and an expression of THE NAME. In the Guide for the Perplexed, Maimonides teaches that the Hebrew Bible's many names for God were all derivative of THE NAME. Isaac the Blind took it a step further. "All language," he posits, "derives from one source: THE NAME."[195]

An anonymous Kabbalistic work from early thirteenth-century Provence revisited the question, How could the two aspects of God, male and female, be one? Rabbi Judah had given his answer (like "wine-soaked bread"). Maimonides had given his answer ("two in some respects, and yet they remained one"). The anonymous Book of Speculation explains it this way: God is paradoxically both "in a state of balanced unity" and at the same time "without compound or distinction."[196] This is reminiscent of Sefer ha-Bahir, in which God is paradoxically two distinct aspects clinging to one another (*davek*) and two aspects that are utterly united in their essence (*miyuchad*).[197]

The Book of Speculation also hints that the letters of THE NAME need to be reordered. Borrowing a phrase from Proverbs 25:11, the Book of Speculation describes THE NAME as "a word spoken on its revolutions" (*davar davur al-ofnav*).[198] Another anonymous work of the same period, the Explanation of the Four-Lettered Name (Perush Shem shel Arba Otiyyot) also hints that the key to understanding THE NAME is to be found through backward writing. This work tells a story involving the prophet Jeremiah, who receives an instruction to "write the alphabets with intense concentration backwards."[199]

Isaac the Blind, careful not to put too much in writing, was acknowledged by the growing circle of Kabbalists as their leader. Later Kabbalists would call the reticent rabbi the father of Kabbalah.[200]

Thirteenth Century, Spain

By the early thirteenth century, Isaac the Blind's Kabbalistic teachings had reached Spain. His teachings had been brought there—to the city of Gerona, only about 150 miles from Provence in the northeast corner of Castilian Spain—by his nephew and disciple Rabbi Asher ben David. In no time, the Geronese Kabbalists had disseminated the Master's teachings and had begun to write their own Kabbalistic treatises on THE NAME.

Rabbi Azriel of Gerona (ca. 1160–ca. 1238) taking up the question of how the two aspects of God could yet be one writes: "If the Receptor did not unite with the Bestower into one power, then it would not be possible to recognize that the two are really one." And yet, Rabbi Azriel taught, the so-called male and female potencies are not fixed; they are fluid. God's emanations alternate their gendered roles. "Everything is both Receptor and Bestower."[201]

Rabbi Azriel had been greatly influenced by Maimonides and the other Jewish philosophers, as had all the Spanish rabbis of his generation. From his writing, we can clearly see that Rabbi Azriel was presenting not a theory of God's sexuality so much as a philosophical understanding of the nature of reality that employs the metaphor of sexuality.[202] God is the coming together, "the synthesis of everything and its opposite." Wherever we see two, "the two are really one" because "nothing exists outside" of God.[203] Here again is the ancient philosophical doctrine taught by Heraclitus, the unity of opposites.[204] The fifteenth-century Nicholas of Cusa (whose reputation in Jewish circles is tarnished because he ignobly advocated for a law requiring Jews to wear a distinctive yellow patch) would later be credited with giving name to a similar principle, the *coincidentia oppositorum*.[205] The Kabbalists had their own name for it: *ha-achdut hashvaah*, the unity of equals.[206]

And yet the Kabbalists were not fundamentally philosophers. They were not interested in the idea of unity alone; they were more interested in the experience of unity. Toward that end, another thirteenth-century Spanish Kabbalist, Rabbi Jacob ben Jacob ha-Kohen of Soria (later of Segovia), offers what today reads like a guided meditation: "Concentrate on the image of the letter *alef* . . . Gaze at the form of the letter *dalet*."[207]

In the second half of the thirteenth century, Jacob ben Jacob ha-Kohen taught a spiritual practice known as a *kavvanah*. A kavvanah (a religio-mystical practice observed to this day) is the setting of an inner spiritual intention before speaking or acting—specifically before prayer or the performance of a religious ritual act—in which the words about to be said or the actions performed are dedicated to the unification of God's male and female aspects: "Behold we unite THE NAME of the Holy One, blessed be He, with a perfect heart and a willing soul."[208]

Earlier in the thirteenth century, the Spanish Kabbalist Rabbi Jacob ben Sheshet of Gerona had gone further than anyone before him in hinting at the true pronunciation of THE NAME. Rabbi Jacob ben Sheshet taught that Deuteronomy 6:4 (the verse is known to Jews liturgically as the Shema, the Proclamation of God's Unity) should be explicated "from above to below" and "from below to above"; one explication which "ascends" and another explication which "descends." The Shema states "Hear O Israel YHWH is our God, YHWH is One."[209] If we were to take Rabbi Jacob ben Sheshet's instruction literally and write the letters of the Shema out in a vertical array, we would find that reading it "from above to below" gives us the verse exactly as it appears in the Torah. But reading the arrangement "from below to above," we would twice see THE NAME of God spelled HWHY.

This was an audacious revelation on Rabbi Jacob ben Sheshet's part. Surely he knew that even one uninitiated in the secret would immediately assume the vocalization of HWHY to be *Hu-Hi* ("He-She"). And should anyone question what he was trying to teach here, he goes on to say that "from below to above" was the order of the letters by which Moses read these words: "He began below and concluded above." According to Rabbi Jacob ben Sheshet, Moses read the Shema in reverse. In doing so, Moses would have twice pronounced THE NAME with its letters in the "proper" order, as "He-She."[210]

Was there no end to what these Geronese Kabbalists were willing to reveal? Back in Provence, Isaac the Blind—upon whose teachings the Spanish Kabbalists had relied—was still alive, and he was not happy. Like Rabbi Judah the Pious before him, Isaac the Blind was vehemently opposed to the broad dissemination of the esoteric traditions. In light of what was going on in Gerona, he wrote an angry letter demanding that the secrets remain hidden. It was one thing for a master to privately teach the doctrine to a trusted student. But, Isaac the Blind wrote, "a book which is written cannot be hidden in a cupboard!"[211]

Isaac the Blind's words made a strong impression on Nachmanides (Rabbi Moses ben Nachman of Gerona, 1194–1270). Nachmanides was *the* rabbinic figure of his day. Indeed, Kabbalah came to enjoy such wide acceptance among the Jews of Spain because of Nachmanides's support. But in the face of Isaac the Blind's blistering criticism, Nachmanides decided the situation would be better if he pulled back. He agreed that too much was being revealed. They risked too much by having these teachings floating around, being read by who knows whom and without any oversight or guidance. Someone somewhere was sure to err and take the highly symbolic language literally. Nachmanides had been ready to reveal many more secrets in his Commentary on the Torah. But, so he claimed, he had heard a voice in a dream telling him not to reveal these secrets and so many of his insights were never committed to writing.[212]

A well-known cautionary tale memorialized in the Talmud captured Isaac the Blind's and Nachmanides's sense of dread. The Talmudic tale appears in the midst of an extended discussion in which the rabbis deal with the questions, How much of the esoteric tradition is proper to share publicly, and what of it must be taught only in private? According to the legend, four sages entered the *pardes*, a Persian loanword (and origin of the English word "paradise") literally meaning "orchard." But among the rabbis, the *pardes* stood for the realm of mystical teachings. Of the four who entered the *pardes*, so the story goes, Ben Azzai died, Ben Zoma went mad, Acher "cut the shoots" (a euphemism most likely meaning he became a heretic), and only one—Akiva—entered and departed in peace.[213]

The Kabbalists had been emphatic that nothing they were saying about THE NAME was meant to be taken literally, as described in the words of Jacob ben Jacob ha-Kohen:

THE NAME

> When we say that He wrapped Himself in a white robe [a reference to Psalm 104:2], do not take this literally! For it is known that the Holy One, blessed be He, is not a body nor does He wrap like one of flesh and blood.[214]

Jacob ben Jacob ha-Kohen's brother, Isaac ben Jacob ha-Kohen writes "Neither in all the primordial emanations nor in the next set of emanations is there anything corporeal."[215] But Kabbalah, like all sophisticated thought systems, was subject to misinterpretation. Isaac the Blind had successfully persuaded Nachmanides that the movement had more to lose than to gain by indiscriminately widening the circle of initiates; and the early thirteenth century is marked by that reticence.

Late Thirteenth Century, Spain

By the late thirteenth century, the pendulum had swung again. A year after Nachmanides's death in 1270, Abraham ben Samuel Abulafia (1240–ca.1292) went in a different direction while in Barcelona. He took the position that Kabbalah needed a wider audience and subsequently wrote some twenty-six works that actively promoted its dissemination. Included among them were manuals of meditation on THE NAME and other sacred names. It comes as no surprise that he was severely criticized for this.

In one of his manuals, Abulafia addresses the issue of the "grammatically defective" spelling of THE NAME. As we have previously noted, the four letters of the tetragrammaton when spelled in reverse and properly vocalized produce the sound equivalents of the Hebrew pronouns "He" and "She" (*Hu* and *Hi*). But the letters do not produce the words "He" and "She" precisely as they are spelled in Hebrew. To do that, the silent letter *alef* would need to be added to each of the pronouns.

In his work Light of the Intellect (Or ha-Sekhel), Abulafia accounts for this grammatically defective spelling of THE NAME:

> You will ask me: if it is the case (that the letters *Aleph*, *He*, *Waw* and *Yod* constitute the actual name of God),

why then is this name not indicated as the name of excellence? In fact that would have been appropriate. But because God desired to conceal his name, in order, thereby, to put to the test the hearts of his initiates and also to purify, cleanse and clarify their intellectual capability, it was consequently necessary to keep it hidden away and concealed.[216]

With these few lines, in response to an unnamed interlocutor's question, Abulafia adds meaningful testimony regarding the spelling and meaning of THE NAME. Should someone argue that the letters of the tetragrammaton as we have them cannot be arranged to properly spell out the pronouns "He" and "She," Abulafia would answer that this was done to keep THE NAME secret. (The biblical commentator Rashi had, already in the eleventh century, made general note of the scriptural phenomenon of the "disappearing" letter *aleph*: "We have many words in which an *aleph* is omitted.... Scripture is not particular about omitting it.")[217]

For all he was willing to reveal, Abulafia stops just short of revealing that THE NAME is meant to be read in reverse. But he offers the broadest of hints. Abulafia cites a verse from Deutero-Isaiah: *Hagidu ha'otiot l'achor v'nayda ki elohim atem*. The verse is usually translated along the lines of the King James Bible into something like, "Show the things that are to come hereafter, that we may know that you are gods" (Isa 41:23). But that is not what the words literally mean. Abulafia cites the verse, no doubt, because of its literal meaning: "Pronounce the letters backwards, and We shall know that you are god(s)."[218] He means the letters of THE NAME. Abulafia further gives us an incantation for love utilizing an elaborate mystical name for God: "Let him pronounce [this particular mystical name] frontward and backward."[219] He leaves it to his readers to apply the backward reading to the four-letter name.

Abraham Abulafia is considered one of the greatest Kabbalists to have ever lived. And Abulafia's greatest student, in turn, was the Castilian Kabbalist Rabbi Joseph ben Abraham Gikatilla (1248–ca.1325). Gikatilla is the author of, among other works, the Gates of Light (Sha'are Orah), a treatise on God's names.

Gikatilla opens the Gates of Light by castigating those who would misuse THE NAME "for magical application."[220] Gikatilla's teacher, Abraham Abulafia, had penned his own screeds calling out the Masters of THE NAME for the same reason; as Judah Halevi had centuries earlier. Now Gikatilla took his turn, saying, "How could a mortal conceive of using His Holy Name as an axe is used for hewing wood?!"and "If they [the Masters of THE NAME] say 'Come along and we will give you the Names and incantations which can be practically employed,' my son, do not go along with them."[221]

Gikatilla was not saying that one should not strive to know THE NAME and other holy names in the Torah, all of which, he taught, were "intrinsically tied to the Tetragrammaton."[222] One should with all one's might and to the best of one's ability learn the true names. For those who are serious about pursuing the matter, he offers this cryptic suggestion: the "whole secret is hinted at" in Psalm 16:8.[223] The words there are *shiviti* YHWH *l'negdi*, which can be translated to "I have equalized THE NAME opposite me," suggesting that the male and female potencies of THE NAME, which the mystic constantly seeks to put into a state of balance, reveal themselves when THE NAME is read in its opposite direction.[224] But be aware, Gikatilla wrote, that the verse "I will keep him safe, for he knows my Name" (Psalm 91:14) "does not promise safety by merely mentioning His Name, but by knowing His Name. It is the knowing that is most significant."[225]

Gikatilla went on to stress, as others before him had, that we must not take any of this language literally. For example, he explains, "the true essence of the blessed Creator cannot be discerned by any other than Him."[226] Gikatilla calls not taking the language literally "the first rule." "You must believe," he writes, echoing Maimonides, "that aside from the words themselves there is no other similarity between the attributes of God and our behavior."[227]

Having delivered his stern warning against anthropomorphization, and after putting his readers on notice that the longstanding prohibition against the pronunciation of THE NAME was still in effect, Gikatilla closes the introduction to his Gates of Light with these words: "We must now go forth and explain each of the

Holy Names as they are written in the Torah. . . . And when you grasp this message then you will succeed in your ways, and you will be enlightened."[228]

Gikatilla then goes on to explicate the many names of God found in the Torah. He focuses on the idea of the good name, by which many Jewish mystics were known, such as Gikatilla's close friend Moses ben Shem Tov de Leon. *Shem Tov* means "good name," and the *Ba'alei Shem*, the Masters of THE NAME, would increasingly be called from Gikatilla's time forward *Ba'alei Shem Tov*, "Masters of the Good Name"—perhaps in reaction to the bad press they had received from Judah Halevi and Gikatilla himself. Gikatilla wanted us to consider what, in this context, the word "good" means.

Gikatilla's answer is not what we might expect: in the Torah, he tells us, the word "good" means "unseparated." God saw that the light on Day One of Creation was good (tov, Genesis 1:4).

> But good (*tov*) "is not mentioned on the second day because it is the essence of difference and separation." Regarding the separation of the waters (Genesis 1:6–7), Gikatilla comments, "Wherever there is distinction and separation, good (*tov*) is not to be found, for good (*tov*) comes to bring peace and connect all things.[229]

God's *Shem Tov*, Gikatilla teaches, is God's unseparated name. And the unseparated aspects, coupled together in THE NAME, are, as we have now repeatedly seen, the male and female aspects of God.

Sefer Ha-Zohar

The Book of Splendor (Sefer ha-Zohar), known as the Zohar hereafter, appeared in Spain in the late thirteenth century. Jews were well established in Spain by then, having been there since the time of Titus (d. 81 CE)—although some legends place their arrival much earlier than that. The thirteenth century falls within what Muslims call the golden age of Spain. For Christians, the golden age there would not begin until 1492. Jews debate whether Spain ever had one. If Spain had a golden age it was spotty, relative, subject to stunning reversals, never quite 24-karat, and, without question, definitively over well before the calamitous thirteenth century. By the late thirteenth century, the Jews of Muslim Spain had lived through the Berber sacking of Córdoba in 1013; the fall of the relatively tolerant Umayyad dynasty in 1031; the massacre of the Jews of Granada in 1066; and a succession of increasingly fanatical dynastic rulers: the Almoravids in 1070 and, in the following century, the Almohads, who shuttered synagogues and forced conversion on their Jews upon pain of death.

Meanwhile, the Jews of northern Spain were by the thirteenth century living among Christians who had been waging their *Reconquista* ("reconquest") against the Muslims of the south for hundreds of years. The Christians had been increasingly successful in this campaign and, with regard to the Jews in the area, were growing increasingly, vociferously intolerant. The Fourth Lateran Council of 1215 required the Jews to wear distinctive marks on their clothing. In the midthirteenth century, friars, on the authority of the pope, began to wage a sermon campaign against the Jews. Jews would have to sit through diatribes in their own synagogues on their holiest days, where they were berated for their blindness and threatened with conversion or eternal damnation in hell.

Life for the Jews got only worse. In 1250, a charge of ritual murder was levied in Saragossa, and other libels began to spread.[230] In 1263, Nachmanides, the leader of Spanish Jewry, was forced to take part in public disputation, after which he was made to flee Spain. In 1279, news came that 269 Jews had been hanged in England. There seemed to be nowhere to turn.

What was happening? Maybe the world really was coming to an end. Christians had begun predicting the end of the world as their calendar approached the year 1000.[231] That year came and went, but the millennial generation of Christians and their descendants maintained their Messianic fervor. Early Kabbalah had downplayed Jewish messianism.[232] But Jewish attitudes were changing.

According to Maimonides, 4,938 years had passed since the Creation.[233] That was news to his contemporaries. Jews had not been used to tracking the years this way. All of a sudden, Jews had a way to number the years. Maimonides's calculation was universally accepted throughout the Jewish world (and to this day is the basis for the reckoning of the Jewish year).

By Maimonides's summation, 1240/1241 CE was the beginning of the sixth millennium (the year 5000 on the Jewish calendar). That was important because a Talmudic tradition, attributed to Rav Ketina, had it that the world would exist for only six thousand years "and one [thousand years, the seventh millennium] it shall be desolate."[234] Kabbalistic speculation held that in the sixtieth year of the sixth millennium, or 1299/1300, the female presence of God, the Shekhinah, would arise.[235] The "springs of wisdom"—necessary to prepare the world for the Messianic era—would not open until 1839/1840; the cosmic Sabbath itself—the Messianic era—would not begin until 2240/2241.[236] But at the very least, the beginning had arrived.

And so perhaps the time was right to reveal more than had ever been revealed about the secret of THE NAME.[237] Around the year 1280—forty years into the sixth millennium—Moses ben Shem Tov (Moses son of "Good Name") de Leon began distributing, piecemeal, portions of his voluminous work the Zohar.

We have good reason to believe that Moses ben Shem Tov de Leon not only published the work but also wrote the main body of it as well. One reason is the fact that after he died, his wife and daughter reportedly said that he had.[238] The work was wildly popular. The Zohar took the Jewish world by storm.

What was the appeal of this book? First of all, the genre was completely new. The Zohar is a mystical historical novel. It presents itself, in the main, as a collection of discussions—loosely organized around the Jewish lectionary, the weekly schedule of Torah readings. The dialogue supposedly took place among the eminent second-century Palestinian Rabbi Shimon bar Yochai, his son Eleazar, and a collection of friends and disciples including Rabbi Abba, Rabbi Yehudah, and others.

But more than the genre was new. Early works of Kabbalah hinted that God has metaphorical male and female aspects. But in the Zohar, we find more than hints and acknowledgement. In the Zohar, the male and female aspects of God, and the love relationship between them, *is* the story. This book describes the desire of the male and female aspects of God for each other in ways that can only be described as erotic. More than that, the Zohar insists that when one strips away the narrative level of the Torah and sees past the "garment" the Torah is wearing, one sees that everything in the Torah—indeed, in the Zoharic world-view, and universe—is telling one and the same story, which is about this cosmic desire and sacred coupling (*zivvuga kadisha*) of the Holy Father and Holy Mother.

The Zohar is an audacious reinterpretation of an earlier Jewish mystical tradition, which was itself an interpretation of the ancient notion of a dual-gendered God, prismed by the Zohar through the lens of male-female romantic love. We hasten to point out that although the Zohar draws on older traditions, the Torah at times takes an even broader view of gender and sexuality than the Zohar does. For instance, the Torah depicts Joseph wearing a *k'tonet passim*, a striped, ornamented, or multicolored cloak that is described elsewhere in the Hebrew Bible as the garment worn by a king's virgin daughters (*b'not ha'melech ha'b'tulah*).[239] The Torah suggests a homoerotic relationship between Judah and Hirah.[240] The Torah's widely misunderstood prohibition against an *ish* lying with a *zachar* is not a prohibition against a "man" lying with another "man" (as is often mistranslated) but rather a prohibition against a "husband" (implicitly understood as heterosexual) lying with a "male."[241] But the Zohar appeared in Spain during the age of the troubadours, when the highest and most popular art form of the time was the poetic idealization of heterosexual romantic love, and the author took this trope and ran with it.

Everything in the Zohar is seen through this erotic heterosexual prism: it describes male and female waters (rain and seas), tribes, and letters.[242] Although none of this, as we have been repeatedly told, is meant to be taken literally. And lest we think we can take a simplistic message from all this, what the Zohar considers male and female is always in flux. An angel will sometimes be male and other times female, as can bread and the blade of the "ever turning sword" guarding the Garden of Eden.[243] The Zohar repeatedly teaches "All is one, male and female" and "Male and female, a single mystery."[244]

The Zohar uses "male" and "female" to describe functions, not roles defined by or limited by gender. "Male" in the Zohar is used to designate bestowal, "female" to designate reception. God is, and does, both, which is why the Shekhinah, the feminine aspect of God, is sometimes called "King."[245] The Zohar cryptically adds, "Just as She is called by the name of the male, so He too is called by Her name."[246]

Humans also are and act like both genders, the suggestion being that when a man studies, listens, takes on another's troubles, or consumes a meal he is "female." When a woman teaches, weaves, produces pottery, gives birth, nurses, or sings, she is "male," so to speak. And the great mystery is that all is one.

The Zohar says that "a human is [both] male and female, and is otherwise not called human."[247] It prescribes, "[E]very human being should manifest as male and female."[248] The sin of Adam was that he ruined the marriage between the feminine and masculine halves of God by divorcing himself from his feminine side. When souls issue from heaven, "they issue male and female, as one; [it is only] as they descend that they separate."[249] In seeking to reflect God, a person should strive to be "male and female in town; male and female in the countryside."[250] The Zohar also warns that "any image not embracing male and female is not fittingly supernal," and "Blessings abide only in a place where male and female appear as one."[251] And on and on.[252]

According to the Zohar, certain times are reflective of this underlying unity. For instance, the night of the annual spring holiday the Festival of Weeks (*Shavuot*) is "the night when Bride is joined with Her Husband."[253] So, too, Friday night, the weekly Sabbath evening, is "the time of coupling" of the male and female aspects of God.[254]

When one prays on these occasions—ideally on all occasions—one should not try to beseech or even praise God but to unify God. That, according to the Zohar, was the original liturgical reason for the recitation of the Shema (Deuteronomy 6:4), so "that male and female would join as one."[255] One recited the Shema to "unify the Holy Name."[256]

The Zohar radically reimagines the very purpose of prayer. When Jews stand erect to pray the Standing Prayer (*Amidah*), in that moment when "we rise in the presence of the Supernal King ... male unites with female."[257] Prayer, in its deepest sense, is neither praise nor petition, but the "mystery of unification through mystery of worship," and the "mystery of two names merging into one."[258]

The Zohar never overtly names these two names "He" and "She." But, as in the earlier works of Kabbalah, it drops hint after hint that THE NAME should be read backward. Regarding the opening words of the Torah, Rav Hamnuna Sava is quoted as saying, "We find the letters backwards."[259] Rabbi Shimon says that God's command to Noah, "Come ... into the ark!" hints at the mystery of "reversal of letters."[260] Regarding the biblical character Er, Rabbi Eleazar explains that the meaning of his name is understood when one reverses the letters.[261] Rabbi Chiyya goes so far as to note that in the story of Jacob and Esau, the same two letters appear in one direction in one word and in the opposite direction in another word.[262] Psalms 32:7, according to Rabbi Yose, "is orderly and backward, in either direction."[263]

Was the Zohar revealing too much or perhaps not enough? The Zohar quotes Rabbi Yose as saying, "Blessings settle upon everything kept concealed."[264] Once a secret is revealed, "an opening is provided for the other realm [the reference is to the demonic] to dominate it."[265] But the Zohar's main character, Rabbi Shimon, was much more ambivalent. Over and over in the Zohar, Rabbi Shimon is heard to cry, "Woe is me if I speak! Woe is me if I do not speak!"[266]

How much should be revealed and how much should remain concealed? In years to come, the rabbis would continue to struggle and disagree. The issue was never settled. Historical circumstances would tip the balance in one direction and then in the other. The secret of THE NAME would continue to be taught but in veiled language (albeit in less and less heavily veiled language). Finding new ways to hint at the secret became, for the Kabbalists, a kind of holy art, as well, perhaps, as a way of establishing their credentials and letting each other know that they knew.

The thirteenth- and fourteenth-century Torah commentator Bachya ben Asher for instance, scoured the Torah to find and make note of every four-word cluster from the beginning of Genesis through the end of Deuteronomy where the initial letters of each four-word cluster spell out THE NAME in reverse.[267] Bachya ben Asher never tells the reader why he has gone through the considerable trouble to do this. He did this, of course, as a way of reaching out to the expanding circle of Kabbalists, letting them know that he knew about the importance of the letters *yod heh vov heh* in reverse—the proper spelling of THE NAME.

CHAPTER 6

Coming Home: 1492–1948 CE

Pressure makes diamonds. In the years following the 1492 expulsion of the Jews from Spain, a small circle of Kabbalists—exiles from Spain and Portugal and their immediate descendants—gathered in Sefad, a little hillside town in northern Palestine. There they created the crown jewels of Kabbalah: songs, poems, and prayers, all directed—in a completely open way that would have been wholly unimaginable in an earlier generation—to the female aspect of God.

The years leading up to the expulsion from Spain had been dreadful. In the words of the historian Simon Schama, over those years an "entire pan-European madness took hold of the popular Christian imagination."[268] In Spain, Jews had been accused of plotting to desecrate the Eucharistic host. Panicked mobs accused Jews of bringing the Black Plague and rioted against them in Toledo in 1349.[269] In 1367, again in Toledo, almost a thousand Jewish homes had been burned to the ground.[270] In June of 1391, the Jews of Seville had been attacked; thousands were killed, "their bodies heaped on the streets.... Screaming women and children were pulled by the hair to baptism; those continuing to resist were sliced at the throat."[271] The Spanish Inquisition, initiated in 1478, was at first aimed at rooting out heretics which included suspected insincere Jewish-born converts to Christianity. Unconverted Jews were, at first, not targeted. As dreadful as the years leading up to the expulsion were for the Jews, we can see only in retrospect—knowing what we know today of King Ferdinand and Queen Isabella's Grand

Inquisitor Tomás de Torquedmada's plan for the Jews' total elimination from Spanish society—that expulsion was inevitable.

The expulsion changed everything. Jews had lived in Spain for at least 1,500 years, since before the time a Christian had ever set foot on the Peninsula and well before there had even been an Islamic faith. How could this be happening? In the minds of some Jews, it could only mean one thing: the convulsions the Jews were experiencing could be only the "birth pangs" of the Messiah.[272] And as that idea grew, so did the belief that the revelation of Kabbalistic secrets—chief among them the secret of THE NAME—was not only permissible, but now required. As one unknown Kabbalist wrote:

> The decree from above that one should not discuss Kabbalistic teaching in public was meant to last only for a limited time—until 1490. We then entered a period called "the last generation," and then the decree was rescinded, and permission given. . . . And from 1540 onward, the most important *mitzvah* [commandment] will be for all to study it in public, both old and young, since this, and nothing else, will bring about the coming of the Messiah.[273]

But why did it have to unfold so painfully? The Sefadian Kabbalists would soon take up that question (their answer was that a cataclysmic accident had happened at the creation event). What would happen to evil in the world once the Messianic age arrived? People had long held different opinions about that, some Kabbalists holding to the view of Isaac the Blind that in the Messianic age, because everyone and everything contained a spark of God, all—even Samael, the angel of death—would be redeemed.[274] Theologians call this doctrine *apocatastasis*.[275]

In Sefad, the time had come to openly welcome the Shekhinah, the female aspect of God, whom the Kabbalists believed was ascendant again, to reunite Her with the male aspect of God. This act would begin to balance, once more, the energies of the universe. Toward that end, every Friday afternoon, the Sefadian Kabbalists would dress in white and parade out of doors—as if a band of bridesmaids—to welcome the Shekhinah, honored in song as the "Sabbath Queen" (*Shabbat ha-Malka*). They would escort Her to meet Her bridegroom, the male aspect of God, honored in song as the "Holy One Blessed Be He" (*Ha Kadosh Baruch Hu*). This "wedding" was reenacted every week on Friday just before sunset. This practice was reinstituted from thirteen hundred years earlier. The Talmudic-era Rabbi Chanina was said to have wrapped himself in a robe every Friday evening, and stood as the sun was setting, chanting, "Come and let us go forth to welcome the Sabbath Queen." Rabbi Chanina's teacher Rabbi Yannai, would chant "Come, O Bride! Come, O Bride!"[276] The Kabbalists of Sefad were not making this up, but rather adding new words and music. One of the Kabbalists, Shlomo ha-Levi Alkabetz, wrote a beautiful wedding hymn for the occasion called "Come My Beloved" (*Lecha Dodi*), which is sung to this day on Friday nights in every synagogue throughout the world.

By the sixteenth century, God's female aspect was, in the Jewish world, a completely open secret. No one was attempting to hide it anymore. The Sefadian liturgy took advantage of this openness. Rabbi Isaac Luria (known as the Ari), an Ashkenazic rabbi who led the community in the final years of his life, was so creative that his theology is today considered almost a separate genre of mysticism, which is called Lurianic Kabbalah. And yet, as with the Sabbath wedding, the Sefadians were not creating their traditions out of whole cloth.

As mystics, the Sefadian Kabbalists placed their emphasis on inner spiritual experience. But their inner spirituality extended to the outer material world. They were interested, of course, in questions such as, What is the proper frame of mind to cultivate when one is praying? But they were equally interested in questions such as, What is the proper frame of mind to cultivate when one is doing a good deed? The Sefadian Kabbalists did not make a distinction.

In the past, the rabbis had acknowledged the concept of kavvanah, or "spiritual intention," but they had downplayed its importance. According to the rabbis of the Talmud, praying and doing good deeds were enough. People should not be burdened with the thought that a lack of proper spiritual intention would make their prayers and deeds not count. But the Sefadian Kabbalists put kavvanah front and center.

And what was the most important kavvanah one could have, whether one was praying or doing a good deed? As we have seen, the highest form of intention was bringing the male and female aspects of THE NAME of God together as one. The Sefadian Kabbalists had their own special term for these intentions (the plural form is kavvanot)—*yichudim,* meaning "unifications." Both the early Kabbalist Rabbi Jacob ben Jacob Ha-Kohen and the Zohar had talked about unifications. But the Kabbalists of Sefad were taking the practice to a new level in suggesting that God's unification was the singular goal of every worthy endeavor.

That the male and female aspects of THE NAME of God need to be reunited seems to fly in the face of the Torah's declaration that God is One. This reunification is certainly paradoxical. But here, the Kabbalists' view of God was not unlike Maimonides's previously cited view of the human being: "two in some respects, and yet they remained one."[277]

How the tradition of *yichudim* reached Sefad is not entirely clear. The Sefadian community leader Rabbi Moses Cordovero is often credited, though he may have learned the tradition from his own student, Rabbi Eliyahu de Vidas.[278] In any event, when Rabbi Isaac Luria took over leadership of the Sefadian Kabbalist community after Cordoveros's passing, Rabbi Luria made the practice of unifications the centerpiece of Jewish life. He would lead the community for two short years, the final years of his life. After his death, his many unification kavvanot—his *yichudim*—were collected and disseminated throughout the Jewish world by his disciple Rabbi Chaim Vital.

Formal Jewish prayer takes place usually three times a day. But the Kabbalists, in their embrace of the male and female God, expanded the times, ways, and means in which one can practice spiritual unification. Some of the unifications were exceedingly complex.[279] But the most daring unification—the one that came closest to utterly laying bare the secret of THE NAME—was also the simplest. This was called *Yichud HaShem,* meaning the "unification of THE NAME." It involved the recitation of a simple formula called *l'shem yichud*, which means "for the sake of the unification."

With this formula, one dedicates a particular prayer or a deed "for the sake of the unification" of the "Holy One Blessed Be He" (the Divine Male, *Ha Kadosh Boruch Hu*) and the "Presence" (the Divine Female, *Ha Shekhinah*). The unification formula declares the speaker's intention "to unite the letters of THE NAME *YH* and *WH*" and bind them in perfect unity. (The formula is recited to this day by observant Jews, for instance before the donning of prayer shawls or phylacteries.)

That revelation was astonishing. It told us explicitly what Rabbi Jacob ben Jacob ha-Kohen's formula had earlier implied: the unification of THE NAME of the Holy One specifically meant the unification of the first two and last two letters of THE NAME. The implication, of course, is that one pair of letters of THE NAME is male and the other female.[280] Because the Babylonian Talmud had long ago revealed that *HW* was a shortened name for God,[281] and given that these letters can be vocalized as *Hu* ("He"), it would not have taken much to figure out that the *WH* in YHWH stood for God's male aspect—and therefore the *YH* stood for God's female aspect. The secret of THE NAME really was an open secret.

The revelation of secrets that had been held for so long added fuel to a firestorm of speculation sweeping the Jewish community in the first half of the seventeenth century that the Messianic era was at hand. And in 1648, a twenty-two-year-old mentally unstable Turkish Jew by the name of Shabbatai Tzvi (1626–1676) saw the opportunity and proclaimed himself to be the Messiah and reportedly began publicly pronouncing THE NAME. (No record attesting to his vocalization is known to exist).

Shabbatai Tzvi's fervent supporter, Abraham Miguel Cardoso (1627–1706) also, by his own account, began publicly pronouncing THE NAME. In one of his works, Cardoso wrote, "I revealed the truth of his great name, the divinity of his Presence (*'elohut shekhinato*), to my colleagues and to my friends in great openness."[282] Cardoso was explicit about God being "male and female":

The Blessed Holy One said to Moses, "My Torah is truth, and thus it discourses about the truth in the matter of my divinity in general and in particular, for the Torah is the general and the particular (*kelal u-ferat*). You have already made known to Israel my divinity in general such that they knew that I am God, the Creator who comprises all the generalities.... And in the future you will notify them of the secret of my divinity in particular (*sod elohuti bi-ferat*), with respect to the fact that I am male and female, I and my *Shekhinah*.[283]

Shabbatai Tzvi's false Messiahship and eventual abandonment had sad consequences for the Jewish community. In its wake, talk of God's dual-gendered nature went underground again. The idea, which had over time become normative in the Jewish world, was once again spoken of in whispers.

Uniting THE NAME: Simple and Complex

And yet more people than ever now knew the secret of THE NAME. Kabbalistically inclined rabbis—who were many in number—continued to attract followers. They studied the classic texts, the Zohar above all others, and continued the practice of unifications, seeking to unite the male and female aspects of God. The Kabbalists disagreed, however, over the forms these unifications should take.

The Jerusalem Kabbalists—heirs to Rabbi Isaac Luria's collection of unifications—continued to practice his complicated forms. In their minds, if every aspect of nature and culture possessed male and female potencies—if letters and bodies of water could be gendered, and if everything "male" was also sometimes "female" and vice versa—one could potentially practice an endless number of unifications to bring the world into a state of spiritual balance.

A community devoted to these complicated unifications was established in 1737 in Jerusalem by Rabbi Gedaliah Hayon. Upon his death in 1751, the leadership of this Kabbalistic yeshivah, Bet El, passed to Sar Shalom Sharabi (1720–1777), who published a prayer book based on these complicated unifications (Siddur Kavvanot ha-RaShash).

Meanwhile in Eastern Europe, Rabbi Israel ben Eliezer (1698 or 1700–1760), who would come to be known as the Ba'al Shem Tov, had begun teaching an extremely simple form of unification.[284] Perhaps the best-known example illustrating how the Ba'al Shem Tov's simple form differed from Rabbi Luria's complicated one is a comparison of their respective intentions (kavvanot) for going to the ritual bath (mikvah).

Ritual immersion is highly symbolic, and both Rabbi Luria and the Ba'al Shem Tov saw it as favorable for the practice of unification meditation. Here, first, is the kavvanah of Rabbi Luria (this passage may be difficult to follow; feel free to read it quickly):

> The Ari taught that before immersing oneself in a *mikvah*, one should meditate on the word *mikvah*. One should realize that the numerical value of the letters which make up the word (in Hebrew) is 151. One should then imagine the divine name *Ehyeh*; and then imagine spelling out each of the letters which make up that name, so that the first letter of the name *Ehyeh*, the letter *aleph*, is now itself spelled out alphabetically as *aleph, lamed, fay*, and that that process should then be continued for each of the remaining letters of the name *Ehyeh*. One should then draw one's attention to the fact that the name *Ehyeh* spelled out this way also has a numerical value of 151, which connects it to the word *mikvah*. One should then meditate on the word *nachal*, meaning stream, and then meditate on the seven "expanded" divine names which make up the supernal stream—*Ab, Sag, Mah, Ben, Yod, Heh,* and *Alef*—and then on the Toraitic divine names associated with them, the first four being associated with YHWH, and the last three being associated with AHYH. One should then notice that in the four appearances of YHWH and three appearances of AHYH the letter *yod* appears exactly seven times. One should then meditate on these seven names, and also on the expanded names, to which one should now add the divine name Yah, producing a total of eight *yods*; each of which has

a numeric value of 10, making the total numeric value of the eight *yod*s 80. One should then realize that the numeric value of the first and last letters of the word *nachal* (stream)—the letters *nun* and *lamed*—is also 80, and that the middle letter *chet* has a numeric value of 8. Then meditate on the eight *yod*s, and, realizing that they appear in two groups—the YHWH group and the AHYH group—then meditate on the number 2. Add this number 2 to the value of the word *nachal* (stream) and you now have a value of 90, which is the numerical value of the word *mayim*, meaning water.[285]

Rabbi Luria then goes on to extend this kavvanah specifically for immersion in a ritual bath in honor of the Sabbath.

And now here is the Ba'al Shem Tov's kavvanah for going to the mikvah: "One should think to oneself 'I am going to the *mikvah*.'"[286]

The Ba'al Shem Tov

The Ba'al Shem Tov had a profound impact on Jewish spiritual life. Elevating simplicity over complexity and making the spiritual accessible, he shifted the emphasis away from practices that only the learned could do, such as studying Jewish law, toward more egalitarian practices, such as singing and dancing.

Often overlooked is that the Ba'al Shem Tov revealed an important piece of missing information regarding THE NAME. Joseph Gikatilla had promoted the teaching that "He" (*Hu*) was one of God's names.[287] It was the Ba'al Shem Tov who, so to speak, let the other shoe drop. According to the testimony of his grandson Rabbi Moses Chaim Ephraim of Sudylkow, the Ba'al Shem Tov had revealed (based on a line from the Passover Haggadah) that "She" (*Hi*) was also one of God's names.[288] For those who were unfamiliar with Shabbatai Tzvi and Abraham Miguel Cordoso's pronouncements in the seventeenth century, this came as a real revelation.

Rabbi Israel ben Eliezer is referred to today as *the* Ba'al Shem Tov, as if no others existed before him,[289] and is remembered for his emphasis on spontaneity and joy, the simplicity of his unifications, and the shift away from the realm of the intellect to that of the body when it comes to unifications.

The Ba'al Shem Tov, in the spirit of Rabbi Judah Halevi, emphasized that knowing how to pronounce THE NAME was not enough. The point of spiritual life is not about amassing keys to break the code or about knowing THE NAME phonetically or intellectually. Life is about experiencing the oneness of the world. Whereas the Lurianic approach to unifying the male and female aspects of God had been highly cerebral (did anyone *really* understand Rabbi Luria's unifications?), the Ba'al Shem Tov wanted to make unifications accessible to ordinary people, no matter their degree of learning. As the Ba'al Shem Tov saw it, the world was in need of unifications that people could accomplish in their everyday lives—small reminders in the course of their everyday lived experience that God, and everything, was one. The Ba'al Shem Tov's motto was, to know God "in all your ways" (*b'chol derachecha*, Proverbs 3:6). His doctrine was "service through corporeality," or "bodily prayer" (*avodah b'gashmiut*).

Within a few generations, the movement he founded, known as *Hasidut*, had factionalized and become religiously conservative in the extreme.[290] The Hasidic movement today is considered an "ultra-Orthodox" movement.[291] But in the Ba'al Shem Tov's day, up to and including the movement's third generation (1809–1815), Hasidisim was marked by a radically new, open approach to religious life.[292] Following traditional rules about when to pray the three daily prayers was less important than the spontaneous spiritual expression one could generate within prayer. Joy was paramount. Nor did one need to sit in the study hall (in fact, the Ba'al Shem Tov taught, study could be an impediment to spiritual awareness). Religious acts, if one was not careful, could be hollow. Meanwhile, the male and female aspects of THE NAME could, with proper intention, be united in the simplest, most mundane acts of everyday life.

In the Ba'al Shem Tov's world-view, eating, drinking, and communing with friends and with nature—all of which human beings are capable of doing by virtue of the fact that we have bodies—are opportunities for unification. Isaac Luria's complicated unifications were still permitted.[293] But the Ba'al Shem Tov minimized their use. In his view, the extreme intellectualization of the Lurianic unifications could actually be more of an impediment than a path to experiencing God's oneness. The key to a spiritual life was the experience of "clinging" to God (*devekut*) and the unification of the divine aspects within one's own body wherever one happened to be. The Ba'al Shem Tov wanted to bring everything down to the human level.

With proper intention, as one lifted one's voice in song, rose for the Standing Prayer, and entered into the waters of the mikvah, one was, in those moments, "male" uniting with "female." With proper intention, as one ate, drank, or took in words of the Torah or a beloved companion, one was, in those moments, "female" uniting with "male."[294] It was as simple as that.

Service of the Body

The Hasidim were especially noted for a prayer practice rooted in the Ba'al Shem Tov's doctrine of service of the body. The prayer practice is called shuckling.[295] For this they would be mercilessly derided.

Shuckling comes from the Yiddish word meaning "to shake." Why would someone shake during prayer? The answer is that, according to the Ba'al Shem Tov, prayer is the consummation of the human-Divine love relationship.[296] And here we understand an important part of Jewish mystical doctrine: unification does not take place only within THE NAME but between THE NAME and the human being.

The Ba'al Shem Tov's disciple Rabbi Yaakov Yosef (1710–1784) of Polnoye, Ukraine, was even more forthcoming about this practice, elucidating the Prayer of Love which precedes the Proclamation of God's Oneness (the Shema).[297]

> The liturgy prescribes that the Prayer of Love must be recited before the Proclamation of God's Oneness. The Master was told that the Messiah has not come because

people do not devote themselves sufficiently to this prayer. These words of love are the kisses that precede sexual union, awakening desire in the Presence so that her child, compassion, might come forth.[298]

We know, of course—because many rabbis have repeatedly stated so—that none of this was to be taken literally. Moreover, a ritual belt (*gartel* in Yiddish) is out of modesty worn during prayer, separating the heart from the lower extremities. And yet this acting out of the symbolic coupling of the so-called male and female aspects of God made the Hasidim scandalous in the eyes of their co-religionist Opponents (*Mitnagdim*). Even Martin Buber, who drew much of his spiritual inspiration from the Hasidic movement, described shuckling as "a sight both grotesque and sublime."[299]

Shuckling is still practiced in some quarters of the Orthodox Jewish world today, even by those who presumably do not understand why. As is widely the case with religious behaviors, the practice of shuckling seems to have been assimilated as if by osmosis. But when understood and practiced with intentionality, shuckling is what scholars of religion call a *theurgic* act; an act believed by the performer to have a direct effect on the divine sphere. In the case of shuckling, the goal is to encourage—even aid if it can be said—the male and female aspects of God to metaphorically mate. Sexual congress being the great metaphor for mystical union, only Moses of all people, according to the Zohar, achieved "intercourse," so to speak, with the female presence of God (the Shekhinah).[300]

Having repeatedly underscored that none of this was meant to be taken literally, I hasten to add that most Jews would still consider the idea—as highly abstract and symbolic as it may be—as far from "mainstream" Judaism as could possibly be imagined. And yet, to appreciate how deeply embedded in Jewish liturgy this motif of the "mating" of God's male and female aspects is, one need only walk into any Jewish service on a Friday night or look in any Jewish prayer book of any denomination, from Orthodox to Reform. Even in the old *Union Prayerbook for Jewish Worship*—which was used through the middle of the twentieth century by German American Reform Jews for whom shuckling was absolutely verboten—we find the words of Alkabetz's mystical wedding hymn "Come My Beloved" (*Lecha Dodi*) that honors the uniting of God's male and female aspects.[301]

All these thousands of years later here it is again: the Sumerian "sacred marriage" of god and goddess; the *hieros gamos* of the ancient Greeks; the belief that a millennia ago gave rise to the practice of cultic religious prostitution; the superstition that had pagan men and women acting out the mating ritual of their gods; the vestigal trace in the modern world of the ancients' belief in sympathetic magic; and the human play intended to stimulate divine copulation, which, according to Gerda Lerner, "may date back to the Neolithic period and to the various cults of the Mother-Goddess."[302] One has to think that very few Jews have the slightest idea where this practice of shuckling came from—that it is rooted in an ancient pagan religious drama intended to mirror the mating of Mesopotamian gods and goddesses. This religious ritual is as old as the hills (certainly as old as the Neolithic cave paintings up in the hills). But the line is direct and incontrovertible.

Shuckling evokes what the Kabbalists called the holy coupling (*zivvuga qadisha*) of the divine King and Queen, the male and female aspects of the One God. Yes, it would be scandalous if people were to take this literally. But the early Hasidim were not taking it literally. If anything, they would have said that they were elevating and "sweetening" the ritual.

The Torah teaches that the human being was created "male and female" in God's image. But what could "male and female" mean in reference to an incorporeal God? What could "male and female" mean if bodies of water and letters were gendered—if everything male was sometimes female and everything female was sometimes male?

The answer, according to the early Hasidim and Jewish mystics who preceded them, is, of course, that it is all metaphor. God is light: "enveloping light" and "penetrating light" (*ohr makif* and *ohr p'nini*) and elsewhere referred to as *sovev* and *mimalei*, or "surrounding" and "filling." The lights ebb and flow, back and forth, running and returning, emptying and filling—sometimes they function in the plural but in reality are only one singular light. And since, according to Hasidism's monist world-view, "everything is God" (*alz ist Gott*), the human being is also everything—neither male nor female; ultimately only light; ebbing and flowing, running and returning, emptying and filling. Humans constantly reflect God and are ultimately inseparable and indistinguishable from God. We are made up of nothing but God—nothing but THE NAME.

Kalonymus Kalman Shapira, the Holy Fire

By the twentieth century—almost a thousand years after Aaron of Baghdad had instructed Rabbi Moses ben Kalonymus of Lucca, Italy—another Kalonymus, Rabbi Kalonymus Kalman Shapira, otherwise known as the Piaseczner Rebbe, was lending his gifted, poetic voice to this numinous, mystical teaching.

Human actions, according to Rabbi Shapira, were capable of uniting the male and female aspects of God known as "Mother" (*Ima*) and "Father" (*Abba*).[303] THE NAME, he taught, is always half-hidden and half-revealed in the world.[304] But if we are sensitive enough, we can unite THE NAME through simple physical acts, such as eating and drinking if, while in those actions we notice how we are drawing sparks of divine energy from the outer physical world and uniting them within the body, our inner physical world. We are even able to unite THE NAME through the simple act of listening, by mindfully noticing and taking in the sounds of the world, "from the twittering of the birds, from the lowing of cattle, and from the voices and cacophony of people."[305]

Nothing was more important, the Piaseczner Rebbe taught, than this unification of THE NAME. Indeed, when we act in ways that unify THE NAME, new heavens come into being. No greater tragedy could be imagined than the tragedy caused, God forbid, by the person who, sundering the world, "disunites the One."[306] THE NAME had given rise to all that is. Out of *YH* God had created the World to Come (*Y*) and the World That Is (*H*).[307] Out of *WH* God had created the possibility for the human being to act freely.[308] Everything was an expression of THE NAME.

And according to the Rebbe, one had to resist the temptation to split the world into good and evil, even in moments when the world was crushing the soul. One had to resist the temptation to see the world as the opposition of angelic and demonic forces. Yes, the demonic forces were twisted, fallen, distorted, perverse, unrecognizable, sick, terrifying—all of that and more. But they were not fundamentally untouchable, unreachable, unredeemable, nor were they the "other." The great teaching of THE NAME was, as he would have said in Yiddish, that *alz ist Gott*—that everything is one, because "everything is God."

Rabbi Shapira's beliefs didn't contain anything extraordinarily new. What was extraordinary about them was where, when, and to whom he was teaching: in the Warsaw Ghetto in the midst of the destruction of the Jewish community to his doomed and desperate disciples.

After the war, a construction worker, preparing a foundation for a new building on the site of what had been the Warsaw Ghetto, found a canister buried in the ground. Inside was a bundle of papers with ATTENTION!!! written in bold letters, followed by three explanation points. The cover letter to the bundle of papers, dated January 3, 1943, instructed the finder of the package to deliver it to an address in Tel Aviv for safekeeping until after the war. The letter was signed Rabbi Kalonymus Kalman Shapira.

The bundle of papers turned out to be the Rebbe of the Warsaw Ghetto's reflections on the weekly Torah portions, written over the course of almost three years from September 1939 through July 1942. He called them "Torah Insights from the Years of Fury," though in 1960 the collection was published in Israel as *Holy Fire* (*Esh Kodesh*).

Poland had been home to Jews for over a thousand years and for centuries been the center of the Jewish world. Polish Jews called Vilna the "Jerusalem of Lithuania." They called their own Crakow the "Little Land of Israel." They had made a wordplay of *Polanya*, the Hebrew word for Poland, saying that it stood for "Here (*Po*) dwells (*lan*) God (*Yah*)." "Torah Insights" would be the last work of Polish Hasidism.

Rabbi Kalonymus Kalman Shapira did not survive the war. Following the Warsaw Ghetto uprising (April 19 to May 16, 1943), Rabbi Shapira was deported to a labor camp, Trawniki, in the Lublin district. And then, nine months to the day after having buried his papers, on November 3, 1943, in an operation dubbed Harvest Festival, he and all the other workers in the camp were rounded up by the Waffen-SS, taken to a nearby training camp, and shot.

How he did what he did—living in the ghetto among all the suffering rather than removing to a safer location when he had the chance; tending to the needs of his beleaguered fellow Jews, many of whom he reports as having gone mad during the course of the bombardments; suffering through the agonizing days-long death throes of his only son, Rabbi Elimelekh, who was struck by a bomb fragment on the morning after Yom Kippur in 1939 and suffering the death of his young daughter-in-law, Git'l, who was felled by a bomb as she waited at the hospital entrance for news of her husband—is beyond imagining; beyond imagining that he could have maintained his belief in THE NAME; maintained his belief that the unification of THE NAME was still possible even in the midst of such unimaginable suffering; maintained his belief that nothing was outside of God; maintained his belief that everything was ultimately nothing more than THE NAME.

And yet, as his biographer Rabbi Nehemia Polen wrote, Rabbi Shapira held to this utopian vision:

> Samael [the angel of death] redeemed, mended, transformed into a force for good, a sacred angel whose desire was now to bless Israel. The persecutors were perpetrating a colossal evil, but the horrific forces they embodied would one day be rectified into a source of blessing. This stance, rooted in hasidic monistic theology, was actually compelled by an inner logic: one cannot fight a demonic force by absolutizing its demonic character; that would merely confirm the demonic view of reality by providing it with a mirror image. To concede that there is indeed a domain of absolute evil that has no contact whatsoever with the possibility of redemption is to succumb to the enemy's own gnostic dualism.[309]

What can be said regarding this level of fidelity to a world-view like his under such circumstances? Certainly, it defies plain sense. This world-view does not easily suggest itself in the extremis of the unfolding events. This belief must have been so deeply woven into Rabbi Kalonymus Kalman Shapira's consciousness that not one more reasonable, alternative explanation could have displaced it. It must have been a belief so much a part of the rabbi's being that letting go of it would have meant letting go of his very self, the deepest truth he knew, and the foundation upon which all meaning rested: that he, and every living being with whom he shared the world—all the so-called male and female elements of every created thing with or without a name, and THE NAME—were one.

CHAPTER 7

Interpreting THE NAME: Yesterday, Today, and Tomorrow

Two and a half millennia have now passed since Ezra ha-Kohain the Scribe carried a Torah bearing stories of THE NAME from exile in Babylonia to the Temple in Jerusalem. It should come as no surprise, given how many years have passed, that different people in different places enduring different circumstances have interpreted THE NAME in different ways.

To Ezra the Scribe of the First Persian Empire period, THE NAME was the unity of opposites, the male-female God in whose image the human (*ha'adam*) and humanity (*adam*) had been created. To Rabbis Chanina and Oshaya of the early Common Era, THE NAME was nature's code—as elemental and vital to them as DNA is to us—that God, and they themselves (so they claimed), had used to create life. To the Masters of the Name (*Ba'alei Shem*) of late antiquity, THE NAME was more than nature's code—its letters were keys to the supernatural, magical entities with which time and space could be made to collapse. To the Kabbalists of the Dark Ages (the author or authors of the Book of Bright Light), the elements of THE NAME had tragically divided, and in the separation of the male and female aspects, the Kabbalists saw their own longing and sorrow. To Maimonides (1135–1204), this was blasphemy. Not only, according to the rationalist Spanish Jewish philosopher, was THE NAME immutably "one," it was "utterly and uniquely" so. That is certainly how Rabbi Eleazar ben Judah of Worms (1165–1230), the last of the mystical German Jewish Pietists, understood THE

NAME—its elements were as indivisible as wine-soaked bread. The Spanish Kabbalist Moses ben Shem Tov de Leon (active ca. 1280) disagreed. In his classic work The Book of Splendor, or the Zohar, de Leon depicted the divided male and female aspects of THE NAME as pining for their eventual reunion. From this story, the Kabbalist Rabbi Isaac Luria of Sefad (the sixteenth-century Holy Ari) created his own full-fledged theological cosmogony—a coherent religious theory of the origin, evolution, and destiny of the universe. Two centuries later, the founder of Hasidism, Rabbi Israel ben Eliezer, the Ba'al Shem Tov, brought THE NAME back to earth, teaching his followers that cosmic unification could be effected here and now by small acts of simple, personal piety. All separations, the Ba'al Shem Tov encouraged his followers to remember, are only apparent separations; no darkness can be said to be completely devoid of light. The secret of THE NAME, he reminded them time and again, is that everything—everything—is one.

Twenty-five hundred years, from Ezra's day to ours, is an enormous expanse of human time. But the inscription of THE NAME at Soleb means that THE NAME had been worshiped at least one thousand years before Ezra.

What might THE NAME have meant to those earliest worshipers? And what—given our historical vantage point, social and scientific knowledge, and altogether different world-view—might THE NAME mean to us today?

What Did THE NAME Mean to Its Earliest Worshipers?

We have no stories about THE NAME that credibly date back to 1400 BCE. The earliest stories we have about THE NAME are believed to have been composed hundreds of years later. And so we are not able to reconstruct exactly what meaning (or meanings) THE NAME might have held for its original, ancient audience. At this, we can only guess.

One can imagine THE NAME as a vestige of polytheism. Perhaps it signified two gods, one male and one female, bound to each other. Or maybe it was a fertility symbol, signifying eternal fecundity, capable, if successfully appeased, of conferring such blessing upon its worshipers.

Or it might be that THE NAME signified a unitive deity—an intersex god believed by its worshipers to be a physical as well as spiritual being endowed with sexual characteristics analogous to human sexual characteristics. Its intersexuality, as the stories would later have it, was the generative source of all things male and female in the world.

Or THE NAME might have meant something much more abstract—the coupling of the pronouns "he" and "she" indicating that God was "everything," this and also that, everything and also its opposite. The poetic term for indicating completeness through a pairing of opposites is *merism*: "I searched high and low" means "I looked everywhere," and "The long and short of it" means "I am telling you everything I know." Perhaps to some of its earliest worshipers, THE NAME meant nothing gendered after all, but everything and no thing. Perhaps it was significant that—even deciphered, composed as it is of pronouns—THE NAME is and is not a name. There really is no way to know.

As for what, if anything, THE NAME might mean to us today, let us consider, without necessarily embracing any of its past meanings, whether we can find a "useable history" here for us. And by "us," I mean all of us—Jew and non-Jew, secular and religious.

I think we can. I can think of at least five ways with which reclamation of THE NAME as dual gendered might help make the world a better place: by (1) making religion more reasonable, (2) helping enfranchise and empower girls and women, (3) supporting the gender revolution, (4) bettering the prospects for world peace, and (5) helping to shape the new modernity.

Making Religion More Reasonable

Religion is unreasonable, at least in many of its iterations—often proudly, sometimes belligerently, even violently so. It should come as no surprise that increasing numbers of people think of religion as something less than purely good, not good, and even the opposite of good.

Of course, no one belongs to "religion." People belong to a *particular* religion, particular *stream* of a particular religion, or a personalized *version* of a particular stream of a particular religion. Vast differences are overlooked when we speak about religion in general.

Religions do have some things in common, and I would hasten to point out that not all of them are the opposite of good. For instance, highly religious people are more likely to donate to charity and do volunteer work than less religious people, according to a Pew Research Center study of American adults:

> Roughly two-thirds of highly religious adults (65%) say they have donated money, time or goods to help the poor in the past week, compared with 41% who are less religious. . . . Adults who are highly religious are more likely than those who are less religious to say they did volunteer work in the last seven days (45% vs. 28%).[310]

One can point to acts of selflessness on the part of religious people and atrocities committed by nonreligious people. Still some would argue that, on balance, the world would be better off without religions.

But these religions are all cultures. In the same way a healthy ecosystem depends on biodiversity, healthy social systems depend on cultural diversity. By engaging with people who see the world differently than we do, we understand ourselves and the world better; we gain more than we lose. Rabbi Jonathan Sacks captured this with his felicitous phrase: the dignity of difference, in his book of the same title.

In any event, religions are not going away. The rituals, traditions, memories, and myths are too powerful for too many people. Billions of people on earth are religious. Even among today's religiously unaffiliated (the so-called nones) religion maintains influence: two-thirds of the religiously unaffiliated profess a belief in God.[311]

Given all that, can we somehow imagine our way toward more "reasonable" religions? Can we imagine religions absent their tribalism, chauvinism, triumphalism, and authoritarianism?

I think we can. I think we can imagine religions in which scripture is not taken literally but is rather approached with reason, skepticism, and curiosity—not as dogma to be denied on pain of excommunication, damnation, or death but as an invitation to think about what is truly meaningful in life. I think we can. In fact, I know we can.

The Kabbalists did not read the Zohar literally. The Jewish rationalist philosophers, such as Moses Maimonides, did not read the Bible literally. The Greek philosophers did not read Homer literally. They all read their respective sacred myths as allegories. They all understood the true meanings of their sacred myths to be found in their undermeanings (or in Greek: *hyponoiai*).[312]

When we say that fundamentalist, literalist readings of scripture are at odds with how scripture was understood by those who knew it best, we are standing on solid ground. Scripture is not in all its respects literally true; and in the ancient world, except in the public imagination, it was never understood to be so.[313] The rabbis were very clear: the Torah was written in a language that an average human being of the time could understand (*b'lashon adam*).

Reading scripture with an eye toward its undermeanings, understanding that the stories in our scriptures are allegories, religious people could let go of creationism and other antiquated and antiscientific ideas. To be sure, symbolic storytelling can produce misreadings. But when we interpret our sacred myths as allegories, we stand in the company of venerated saints and sages.

The writers of the Hebrew Bible composed their metaphors as ways of talking about THE NAME, the central theme of the Hebrew Bible—one that resonates with increasingly many Americans today. This may come as a surprise, but most Americans now reject the idea of God as male. More Americans (42 percent) now believe that God is both male and female, neither male nor female, or female than believe that God is male (39 percent).[314] That's a big deal. Rather than continue to perpetuate a myth that is no longer supported even by religious believers, we could embrace an allegorical language about God that reflects our collective, evolved, reasonable understanding.

Enfranchising and Empowering Girls and Women

For religious traditionalists uncomfortable with welcoming "God the Mother" alongside "God the Father," I would ask you to open your heart to Mary Daly's trenchant observation: "If God is male, then male is God."[315] Whether we aware of or intend it or not, when we speak of God as "He," we are denigrating half the world's population and relegating them to second-class status—or worse.[316] By identifying God with male and not female, we are fostering a highly dysfunctional world-view in which power, privilege, and value have come to be seen as inherent in boys and men, not in girls and women. Beyond the simple personal indignity, this world-view permits—and in fact often promotes—the perpetuation of physical and emotional violence against girls and women.

Women across the world to this day are made subservient to their husbands, beaten, raped, held as chattel, blocked from divorcing their abusers and even subjected to so-called bride burning or "honor" killing—all with religious warrant. No reflective religious person would want this to continue. It would be naïve to think that re-envisioning God as female and male would in and of itself be enough to create the conditions necessary for women's liberation across the planet. But the conscionable action is to do everything we can to reset the norms and check our implicit biases and assumptions that, consciously or unconsciously, we are passing on to our children. The allegory of God's creating humanity male and female in the image of God himself-herself is a story worth telling today.

All the world's religions have work to do to elevate the role of women. Happily, that work is underway. Some movements today seek the ordination of women rabbis in the Orthodox Jewish world and the ordination of women priests in the Roman Catholic and Mormon worlds, as well as acceptance of women prayer leaders in the Islamic world.[317] Perhaps these movements will draw inspiration from the story of THE NAME. Perhaps this old-yet-new understanding of THE NAME will, in ways we cannot expect to trace from here, shift the ground on which decisions about human religious leadership are made and remade.

At the same time, maybe secular women's movements (such as movements for equal pay), while not dependent on religious support, nor necessarily even desirous of it, will yet feel even more wind in their sails.

Supporting the Gender Revolution

Taking the metaphor of THE NAME to heart may help us to rethink gender roles. Over the past few years, the very notion of gender has undergone a revolution in the West. Gender roles of the past are now seen for what they were: traditional—meaning socially constructed—rather than essential—meaning arising out of innate differences. Terms like "woman-lawyer" or "woman-doctor" sound downright bizarre to anyone younger than a baby boomer. Moreover, gender is no longer universally accepted as binary—meaning that one must, or even necessarily can, identify with one of two genders rather than with both or with neither—especially among millennials. We know from an abundance of cross-cultural studies that many societies recognize the existence of more than two genders; the rabbis of the Talmud knew of six.[318]

In urban and suburban middle schools, at least in some parts of America today, students are now routinely being asked for their gender pronoun. It may be "he," "she," "them," or something else entirely. A person's gender may or may not be obvious from their appearance. If one assumes, one could be wrong.

It may be a reach for some older people to get their heads around this, but gender, we now understand, exists on a spectrum, just as sexual orientation and biological sex exist on a spectrum. One's gender identity (or how we seem to ourselves) might be very, moderately, or minimally "manly," "womanly," both, or neither. So, too, gender expression (or how we present to others) runs along a spectrum. At the same time, one might be very, moderately, or

INTERPRETING THE NAME: YESTERDAY, TODAY, AND TOMORROW

minimally heterosexually attracted (straight), homosexually attracted (gay), both (bisexual), or neither (asexual).[319] And biological sex exists on a spectrum as well; it includes an often forgotten population: the intersexed, which occurs in perhaps one in every two thousand babies born.[320] And many more descriptors cover a wide range of possibilities. Increasingly, all of this passes for common wisdom among young people.

Included above, of course, are people who live at a far end of the gender spectrum, people who suffer from gender dysphoria, whose gender identity is out of alignment with the gender they were assigned at birth. Fortunately, there is today greater general understanding and wider social acceptance of transgender people. So-called reparative therapy—which didn't work when foisted on any group of people, including left-handed, gay, lesbian, or transgender people—has lost credence in the scientific world. Trans people—who in a previous generation, before transitioning was an option, would have known anguish and suffering their entire lives—are finding a relatively easier path (emphasis on "relatively").

But transgender is a broad term. It means different things to different people in different contexts. It can be used to refer to someone who has transitioned or plans to transition, via hormone therapy and surgery (the term for this used to be and sometimes still is "transsexual"). But transgender can also apply to people who have not yet undergone or do not plan to ever undergo surgery. It can also apply to someone whose identity "transcends" gender. Language is fluid; the terminology is still evolving.

THE NAME can be interpreted as transgender in any number of ways. I am not arguing in favor of a particular interpretation. But I do find it hopeful that individuals living at different places across the gender spectrum might see themselves and their experiences affirmed in THE NAME.

Bettering the Prospects for World Peace

It might seem like a stretch to argue that an interpretation of THE NAME of God could have any practical bearing on the issue of world peace. But THE NAME contains a powerful message. It suggests that gender equality is a quality of divinity, which is important because public policy analysts have drawn a direct line between gender equality and state security.

Studies have demonstrated conclusively that the enfranchisement of girls and women increases the likelihood that a state will be at peace, and vice versa. In an important work titled *Sex and World Peace*, researchers Valerie M. Hudson, Bonnie Ballif-Spanvill, Mary Caprioli, and Chad F. Emmett share clear and compelling evidence proving that in countries where women and girls enjoy physical security and equity under the law, and where participation of women in decision making is high, the chance that that state will be at war is significantly decreased.[321] To the extent that our understanding of THE NAME as a dual-gendered deity can, even in a small way, help better the odds that social power between men and women will be equalized, THE NAME partakes in an effort that public policy experts tell us has life or death consequences. Indeed, in the dangerous time in which we live, what Hudson et al. call "women's wisdom"—consensus over conflict—may be the only chance humanity has to avert its self-destruction.

And we have reason to be hopeful that we can let go of the long-held misguided belief that men are naturally superior to women. As Gerda Lerner wrote over thirty years ago,

> As long as both men and women regard the subordination of half the human race to the other as "natural," it is impossible to envision a society in which differences do not connote either dominance or subordination.... [But] the system of patriarchy is a historic construct; it has a beginning; it will have an end. Its time seems to have nearly run its course—it no longer serves the needs of men or women and in its inextricable linkage to militarism, hierarchy, and racism it threatens the very existence of life on earth.[322]

Shaping the New Modernity

The gender revolution is not the only revolution going on right now. Nationalism, capitalism, race, and ethnicity are, as well, all undergoing radical reevaluation. Broadly, we can think of this as the unfolding of the "new modernity."

The old modernity was born in the period known as the Enlightenment, and it rested on notions of individuality. Everything, as William Everdell pointed out in *The First Moderns*, was seen as discrete: people (with new individual rights) were discrete; genes, neurons, particles, atoms, and later subatomic quanta were all discrete. The artists of modernism portrayed the world—through their pointillist and cubist works of art—as fundamentally discontinuous.[323]

Then came the period known as postmodernism. Postmodernism rejected modernism's rigid categories. The very notion of discrete individuals and boundaries in nature was demolished. In the postmodern period, nothing had fixed meaning; everything was fluid, relative, and unstable. The scientists of the age were interested not in individual particles but waves—not in atoms but fields. Postmodern art was likewise all about blurring boundaries: texts, performances, and even assembled junk presented as visual art.

Now we are moving into the period that might be called "new modernity." What characterizes new modernity is that it takes into account both our individual, discrete, bounded realities and the larger, fluid, collective, unbounded reality within which those individual realties exist. Scientists and philosophers, when they speak about reality, sound today like the Pietists and Kabbalists of old. THE NAME, the Pietests said, may be likened to wine-soaked bread—utterly, inseparably one. The origin of the universe, scientists tell us, was a singularity—a state prior to the big bang before the elemental forces de-coupled, in which everything was utterly, inseparably one. The Kabbalists taught that we can look either at the "world of separation" or the "world of unity" (both being valid ways of interpreting reality). And now scientists tell us that the world around us can be viewed as either discrete or continuous, depending on what we are looking to find.

Scientists point as an example to the wave-particle duality of light. Light acts like a particle when we are looking for particles and a wave when we are looking for waves, although classical physics holds this to be impossible.[324] One way is not right, the other way wrong. Or take space and time, which are, post-Einstein, understood as two aspects of one phenomenon called space-time.[325] It does not seem possible, and yet there it is. Reality, it turns out, as Maimonides said of Adam and Eve, is "two in some respects, and yet . . . one."

The idea that everything is both discrete and continuous, separate and whole, is at the heart of integral philosophy. This doctrine grew out of the work of Arthur Koestler and was expanded, developed, and given its name by Ken Wilbur. Integral philosophy seeks to map the deeply complex interconnections that bind everyone and everything together as one.

The same theme informs intersectional theory, which is more easily explained through example. I am a straight, cisgendered, Jewish, Caucasian male. But not one of those aspects represents the totality of my identity, nor even all of them together. How they all intersect is equally defining. Moreover, all of them together would still not be sufficient to predict my love of Irish music and African art or the fact that Chinese New Year is, in my home, as important a holiday as the Jewish New Year. Intersectional theorists, such as Kimberlé Williams Crenshaw, who brought the idea to the fore, are changing the way we think about race, gender, ethnicity, and other identity components. Intersectional identity is an idea that finds deep support in the metaphor of THE NAME.

Integral philosophy and intersectional theory sound academic, but they have practical implications in the real-world. Amartya Sen, the Nobel Prize–winning economist, has written persuasively that our ability to see ourselves and each other in all of our complexity, understand our identities as amalgams of allegiances, and recognize that we are "members of a variety of groups—[that] we belong to all of them" is the antidote to mutually annihilating tribalism.[326]

Understanding that each of our identities is a "plural" identity is the beginning of unwinding the destructive, tribalist, us-against-them narratives that we take with us into the world. Realizing that all of us are "both-and," it becomes harder to maintain the fiction that we are inevitably one another's antagonists. When we see ourselves as complex individuals who share along with all other complex individuals in a larger reality, the notion of self softens. We become more tolerant. Violence no longer seems inevitable.

Tribalism threatens us all. Its only rival for the amount of potential harm is runaway individualism, which puts the wants of the individual above the needs of the world. We need another way of speaking about this tension—maybe an allegory for talking about the relationship of parts and whole—because neither tribes nor individuals are inherently good or bad.

A religious group can be thought of as a tribe. But so, too, can a corporation: its sales force, researchers, and profit sharing are the equivalent of hunters, gatherers, and the divvying up of the kill. A food cooperative can as well, with its farmers, members, and distribution of the harvest. Groups of people with defined roles, responsibilities, and systems of rewards are neither good nor bad, nor is a single person, who can act as a private citizen, independent contractor, or lone wolf.

The new modernity acknowledges the complexity in all of this. It draws wisdom, in part, from the field of psychology, which teaches that human beings have both the need and capacity for individual initiative (agency) and collaborative cooperation (communion).[327] Psychologically, we are wired for both. How well we acknowledge and balance our needs and capacities determines, to a great extent, our psychological health.

So much is riding on our ability to get this right, and draw on our individual and collaborative strengths in the face of economic dislocation, fraying social fabric, climate emergency, and political upheaval. The new modernity offers a framework for thinking it through. But religious myths and metaphors present ideas to people where they already live.

The rabbis drew a lesson from the allegory of THE NAME about individuality and commonality: each and every individual partakes of the world and is a world unto themselves; and no one is more important than anyone else, each person having been stamped with the seal of the original *adam*/earthling that had, itself, been created in the image of God.[328]

Conclusion

THE NAME is the deity that gave rise to the three Abrahamic faiths. The story of THE NAME speaks to the followers of those religions, who today make up more than half the world's population, and hopefully to others as well. Wherever we stand religiously, reflecting on the meaning of THE NAME can only help advance the principle of tolerance for individual differences of global, even cosmic, interdependence implicit within it. Perhaps through such reflection, a more universal embrace of those values will more speedily come to pass.

But all these changes need not occur for at least some good to come. Even if only one of these should come to pass, as the Hebrew Passover song goes, *dayenu*—it would be enough. If only religion could be made more reasonable; if only girls and women could be enfranchised and empowered; if only the gender revolution could be further supported; if only the prospects for world peace could be improved; if only the ideas of tolerance and interdependence implicit in the new modernity could be brought to bear; if only one of these should come to pass, there would be more than enough to celebrate.

How exactly this will play out will be determined by individuals and their communities, secular and religious. It will not all happen at once, nor does it need to happen everywhere in the same way. In the religious world, different communities will find different ways to think about and refer to God that honors girls and women, boys and men. We need not have one name for THE NAME. As the Kabbalists of old said: What is important is not the pronunciation but the understanding of THE NAME.

Afterword

About six months after the publication of "Who Is He? He Is She," as I was beginning to shape that article into this book, I received an email from a member of the Masons of California, a society of Freemasons. This fraternal organization has an interest in biblical symbolism; a reputation for secrecy; and, especially with regard to relations with the Roman Catholic Church, a history of controversy. The writer said that he had read about my discovery and as a Mason he was intrigued. In the nineteenth century, he told me, a theory much like my own—right down to the reverse pronunciation and dual-gender secret of THE NAME—had circulated within the Freemason community. According to Masonic sources, the theory had originated with a renowned linguist and scholar of antiquities—world famous in the early nineteenth century, barely remembered today—by the name of Michelangelo Lanci (1779–1867). Michelangelo Lanci was the Vatican librarian.[329]

Michelangelo Lanci

Born to a noble family in Fano, Italy, Lanci entered holy orders in 1803, and was subsequently ordained a priest. His career at the Vatican began in 1820 when he was appointed professor of sacred philology and made the official interpreter of what were then called Oriental languages for the Vatican.[330] In addition to being a philologist—fluent in Greek, Hebrew, and Arabic, among other languages—Father Lanci was a poet. He had a bachelor's degree in education, master's degree in fine arts, doctorate in theology, and law degree.

But by 1827, only seven years after assuming his Vatican office, his *Sacred Scripture* (*La sacra scrittura*), published with the financial support of the duc de Blacas, had been "entirely suppressed by order of the Pontifical Government, and not more than three copies were distributed."[331] Lanci had declared his audacious agenda on *La sacra scrittura*'s opening page, choosing for the inscription there a line from Psalm 118: "*even ma'asu ha'bonim hai'ta l'rosh pina*," meaning "the stone which the builders have rejected has become the cornerstone."[332] What Lanci was building with this rejected cornerstone was, at least outside the Jewish world, an entirely new understanding of scripture. No wonder the work was suppressed.

Lanci begins by announcing his intention to undertake an analysis of divine names, focusing at first on the divine name Elohim. Elohim, Lanci informs his readers—as Rashi, the eleventh-century biblical commentator had earlier noted—is a plural that is treated grammatically as if it were singular. And, he notes, "grammatically it admits the union of the third person singular, masculine, feminine."[333] He would have much more to say on this theme of conflated gender in his next work, the manuscript of which he began sharing with a group of trusted readers four years later, in 1831.

In this new work in progress, Lanci revealed his analysis of the tetregrammaton and the secret of its dual-gender nature. Don Francesco Vargas, an early reader of that manuscript, would later write, "What one notes most in this praiseworthy manuscript you are seeing is the admirable discovery of the secret of the Tetragrammaton's divine bi-form name, now for the first time explained and demonstrated by our skilled philologist."[334]

When the four letters of the tetragrammaton are reversed, according to Lanci, it reveals two monosyllables, "the first of which is a masculine pronoun, the second a feminine . . . Ho-Hi."[335] In the feminine syllable is to be found "sweetness, gentleness, love, protection, peace, life," and in the masculine syllable, "severe feelings of

AFTERWORD

strength and pride, devastation, war and terror, death and desolation." And, Lanci writes, "in their bi-syllabic totality the adverse compound male and female powers are strongly locked."[336]

Lanci went on to look at some difficult sections of the Hebrew Bible through this lens. Psalm 68 (because it states that God's name is "Yah") was, in his words, a *"scoglio di tutt'i comentatori,"* a stumbling block for commentators. But, he explained, the divine name "Yah," which appears in verses 5 and 19, is the reverse of the feminine syllable *hi*.[337]

Lanci offers comments on the phrases "Your right is valiant" (Psalm 118:6) and "Your right shall overtake those that hate you" (Psalm 21:9). When the tetragrammaton is spelled in reverse, Lanci notes, *Ho* is on the right. And *ho*—the masculine syllable, Lanci tells us—is, in his words the *"simbolo della giusta vendetta, della terribilità, della morte,"* or "the symbol of revenge, of awefulness, of death."[338]

In the tetragrammaton are locked together the feminine pronoun—the *simbolo la felicità*, or the symbol for happiness—and the male pronoun—the symbol for *tormentare*, or torture.[339] The "two mysterious syllables of Hi and Ho . . . are emblems of benefit and punishment, life and death, creation and destruction, and all that is between them, as light and darkness face each other."[340]

All of this was profoundly heretical. If the Hebrew God was dual gendered, then the Christian God was dual gendered—they were the same God, were they not? But in 1845—fourteen years after having first set his theory down in writing—he managed to publish his book *Chronicles (Paralipomeni)* in Paris.[341] This work was officially banned by the Vatican.

The following year, on June 16, 1846, a new pope was elected, who seemed even more determined than his predecessors had been to root out suspected heresy in the ranks. One of the first official acts undertaken by Pope Pius IX was to issue an encyclical entitled *Qui pluribus* (referred to in English as *On Faith and Religion*, but also sometimes *On Faith and Reason*). In the encyclical, dated November 9, 1846, the new pope expressed his "great disquietude and anxiety" to be assuming the office in this "period of great instability." At times he seemed almost to be addressing Lanci directly.

"Ravening wolves," the pope warned, were at that moment seeking "to import the doctrine of human progress into the Catholic religion ... enemies [who] never stop invoking the power and excellence of human reason." The pope took specific aim at "those secret sects who have come forth from the darkness to destroy and desolate both the sacred and the civil commonwealth." He condemned as well "the crafty Bible Societies" and their "perverse explanations," referring ominously to "bitter enemies of the Christian name," men whom the new pope decried as being "carried wretchedly along by some blind momentum of their mad impiety; [who] go so far in their rash imagining as to teach without blushing, openly and publicly, daring and unheard-of doctrines, thereby uttering blasphemies against God . . . enemies of divine revelation . . . [who] attempt to destroy faith . . . subjecting it in an impious manner to reason and changing the meaning of the words of God . . . the result of the unbridled license to think, speak and write."[342]

Letter to Monsieur Prisse

Despite his troubles with the Vatican, Lanci was still regarded as "the world's foremost living Semitic lexicographer," "the profoundest Semitic scholar of the age," and even "the most learned man in the world."[343] Lanci had been studying Egyptian hieroglyphics for twenty years when the world's foremost Egyptologist, Émile Prisse (Achille-Constant-Théodore Émile Prisse d'Avennes), sought him out for an exchange of ideas.[344]

Lanci wrote *Letter on the Interpretation of Egyptian Hieroglyphics, Addressed to Monsieur Prisse of Avennes* (*Lettre sur l'interprétation des Hiéroglyphes Égyptiens, adressée à M. Prisse d'Avennes*) in June 1846 (the month of the new pope's election). In it, Lanci recapitulated his theory of the dual-gendered tetragrammaton. (The word "letter" may give the modern reader the wrong impression. The work is, in fact, a two hundred and three page book, complete with plates.) When *Letter to Monsieur Prisse* was published in Paris in

AFTERWORD

1847, it would bring Lanci's theory of the dual-gendered tetragrammaton to a wider international audience.

Émile Prisse had been appointed successor to Jean-François Champollion—who had first deciphered the hieroglyphic code of the Rosetta stone—upon Champollion's death in 1832. Prisse was awarded the French Légion d'honneur in 1845. And so in Lanci's *Letter to Monsieur Prisse* readers were privy to an address by one of the world's most celebrated scholars in the world to another.

In *Letter to Monsieur Prisse,* Lanci declares that he had "irrefutably demonstrated" that "Moses placed the secret of *Ho-hi* and *Hi-ho* in the double inscription of Jeoa."[345] Lanci believed that answers to more secrets were to be found in Egypt. "May the new interpretations contained in this letter," Lanci concludes, "help you, Sir, in the arduous search you are undertaking in the Valley of the Nile, which you have already explored to the great benefit of science."[346] This work was also officially banned by the Vatican.

In 1848, a year after *Letter to Monsieur Prisse* was published in Paris, the French Revolution touched off a wave of revolutions that would sweep over the entire continent in just two years' time. The pope had been right that those upholding the old order had much to be worried about. About this tumultuous period, Alexis de Tocqueville would later write that society had been cut in two: "those who had nothing united in common envy, and those who had anything united in common terror."[347]

The factors stirring people were many and complex. Tocqueville's comment notwithstanding, not all the factors were economic. Nationalism, liberalism, socialism, and democracy—all the new movements of the day—were founded on the principles of the Enlightenment. And as the Enlightenment had elevated reason and the scientific method above religious dogma, the church found this period deeply threatening. Rightly so. Terrorist acts became common. The pope's Minister of the Interior Pellegrino Rossi was only one of many assassinated. In 1848, the pope himself had to flee Rome for a time.

The Writings of Charles Chauncey Burr

Lanci's theory was first publicized abroad in 1848. A review of Lanci's *Letter to Monsieur Prisse* was published by Charles Chauncey Burr in the January 1848 edition of the American quarterly *Nineteenth Century*.[348] Burr called the results of Lanci's investigations "certainly startling and unexpected, but supported, as they are, by an extraordinary erudition they cannot but command a patient and impartial hearing." He goes on to evaluate Lanci's claims:

> His great work, the *Sagra* [sic] *Scrittura Illustrata*[349] . . . was condemned by Papal authorities and suppressed; so that copies of it are extremely rare. . . . In the fifteenth section [of this new work], he comes to the consideration of the Hebrew tetragrammaton, as illustrated by the Egyptian. . . . The word is Jeoa, or Ihoh, and consists of two vowels, each followed by the same consonant or aspirate, which may be represented by our H. When the reading of this word is reversed, it may be given in our letters as HO-HI. The "secret of the name" probably lay in its being read left to right, contrary to the usual method of Hebrew writing, as well as in the androgynous nature indicated by it. . . . [T]he word IHOH contains the expression of HE-SHE, or the male and female natures included in one being. The first part, HO, is masculine, and the second, HI, is feminine. . . . There is reason to suppose, that the meaning of the tetragrammaton was occult, while the world [sic] itself was common. Ps. cxxxix. 4–6, probably refers to this. Ps. cxi. 1 says:—"I will celebrate IHOH with all heart, in the secret of the righteous and in the congregation:"—that is, among the initiated, and also in public, or esoterically and exoterically. . . . The prohibition of "taking the Lord's name in vain," Lanci thinks . . . would have an exoteric and esoteric sense. To the people it would appear a prohibition of the unnecessary or profane use of IHOH, while by adepts it would be recognized as forbidding the enunciation of the name as HOHI. . . . If his opinions are correct, the Bible is the original and most ancient record of a system of dualism, illustrated by a comparison to the

sexual relation, and hidden under a Kabbalistic veil. . . .
As to the truth or falsity of this view, we have no opinion
to express. We merely give it for what it is worth, and as
indicating the course which Biblical exegesis will soon
have to take. It is too important and apparently too well
fortified by facts to be overlooked. It must be either accepted or disproved. . . . [T]he learned world has before
it . . . a most onerous, but most important task.[350]

In his review, Burr mentions that Lanci had stated his intention to give "in another letter to G. R. Gliddon, Esq.—so well known in our country as a learned and eloquent lecturer on Egyptian subjects—an exposition of the hidden meaning of the celebrated Turin papyrus." George Robbins Gliddon, an archaeologist and former United States counsel at Cairo, was one of Lanci's students.

The Writings of Albert Gallatin Mackey

But it seems that Gliddon never published any of Lanci's teachings himself. Rather, he passed on whatever he had learned from Lanci to his friend Albert Gallatin Mackey. Mackey was an American physician. He was also a member of the Masons, the grand lecturer and grand secretary of the Grand Lodge of South Carolina, and a prolific author of books on Freemasonry.[351]

In the 1860 English edition of *A Lexicon of Freemasonry*, Mackey presents the "speculation of Michael Angelo Lanci, one of the greatest Orientalists of the present day, [which] I have at second hand. His great work—intended to be, indeed, an opus magnum—has not been published; and I am indebted for this, as well as many other of his investigations, to my learned friend, George R. Gliddon, Esq., who was a pupil of this illustrious scholar."[352]

Lanci seems to have been relieved of his duties in 1845, but recalled to Rome from France during the papacy of Pius IX. But he never wrote his magnum opus. He died in Palestrina, Italy in 1867, just shy of what would have been his eighty-eighth birthday.

Two years after Lanci's death, Mackey reviewed his theory once again in his comprehensive *The Symbolism of Freemasonry*:

Illustrating and Explaining Its Science and Philosophy, Its Legends, Myths, and Symbols. In it Mackey writes "[T]he latest, and undoubtedly the most philosophical, speculation on the true meaning, as well as pronunciation, of the ineffable tetragrammaton is from the ingenious mind of the celebrated Lanci; and I have already, in another work given it to the public as I received it from his pupil, and my friend, Mr. Gliddon, the distinguished archaeologist." Mackey went on:

> Elsewhere I have very fully alluded to the prevailing sentiment among the ancients that the Supreme Deity was bisexual, or hermaphrodite, including in the essence of his being the male and female principles, the generative and prolific powers of nature. This was the universal doctrine in all the ancient religions, and was very naturally developed in the symbol of the *phallus* and *cteis* among the Greeks, and in the corresponding one of the *lingam* and *yoni* among the Orientalists; from which symbols the masonic *point within a circle* is a legitimate derivation. They all taught that God, the Creator, was male and female.
>
> Now this theory is undoubtedly unobjectionable on the score of orthodoxy, if we view it in the spiritual sense, in which its first propounders must necessarily have intended it to be presented to the mind, and not in the gross, sensual meaning in which it was subsequently received. For, taking the word "sex," not in its ordinary and colloquial signification, as denoting the indication of a particular physical organization, but in that purely philosophical one which alone can be used in such a connection, and which simply signifies the mere manifestation of a power, it is not to be denied that the Supreme Being must possess in himself, and in himself alone, both a generative and prolific power. This idea, which was so extensively prevalent among all the nations of antiquity, has also been traced to the tetragrammaton, or name of Jehovah, with singular ingenuity by Lanci; and, what is almost equally interesting, he has, by this discovery, been enabled to demonstrate what was, in all probability, the true pronunciation of the word.[353]

Mackey shared "the details of this philological discovery," explaining how in Hebrew "the word HO-HI, literally translated, is equivalent to the English compound HE-SHE." Mackey called it "undoubtedly the most philosophical speculation on the true meaning, as well as pronunciation, of the ineffable tetragrammaton."[354]

Some Final Thoughts on Michelangelo Lanci

How had Michelangelo Lanci come upon this theory regarding THE NAME? We don't know. Perhaps he heard the secret from a Jewish convert. Perhaps he had read Kabbalistic books available at the time that openly hint at the secret and then put the clues together and figured it out himself.[355] Perhaps he was privy to the writings of Guillaume Postel (1510–1581), who was the first person to translate the Zohar into Latin. In Postel's *The Treasure of the Prophecies of the Universe* (*Le Thrésor des Prophéties de l'Univers*, published in 1566), he had—almost two hundred years before Lanci—noted that the tetragrammaton contains the pronouns "he" and "she."[356]

What Lanci's relationship with the Freemasons was is unclear. At the very least, he may have had an indirect association through like-minded scholars. But membership in the Freemasons was considered by the Vatican, then as now, beyond the pale.[357] Lanci would not have spoken about it openly.

What happened to Lanci's theory? Outside of a small circle, his ideas are today virtually unknown. Few have ever heard Lanci's name. A portrait of him by the Russian painter Karl Bryullov hangs in the Tretyakov Gallery in Moscow.[358] A bust sculpted by the French artist Louis Marie Lante sits in the collection of the New York Historical Society in New York City.[359] A brief biography, *Cenni Biografici di Michelangelo Lanci* written by Conte Severino Servanzi Collio di Sanseverino and published in 1839, is available from antiquarian book dealers.

Endnotes

Introduction

1. Jerusalem Talmud, Yoma 18b. Babylonian Talmud, Yoma 39b.
2. Babylonian Talmud, Kiddushin 71a.
3. Even in the event of a court case charging blasphemy, witnesses would be directed to testify euphemistically about what they had heard. The eldest among them would then testify privately about what explicitly had been said, according to the Babylonian Talmud, Sanhedrin 56a.
4. A number of theories try to explain why this translation was done. One reason might be that many Jews were living in the Greek-speaking diaspora. A rabbinic tradition memorialized in the Talmud claims the translation into Greek was done by order of Ptolemy II (285–246 BCE). According to this legend, Ptolemy put seventy-two rabbis into separate rooms. As each of the seventy-two translations was exactly the same, Ptolemy knew he had a translation on which he could rely. The work was called the Septuagint, meaning "seventy." Babylonian Talmud, Megillah 9a.
5. The history of the approximation of diacritic marks is complex. The history of vowel marking under the first letter of the word "Adonai" is *chataf patach*—a compound symbol written with a *sheva* followed by a *patach*. The Masoretic vowel marking under the first letter of the tetragrammaton is a simple *sheva*. The decision to use a *sheva* in lieu of a *chataf patach* may have been made in order to prevent accidental pronunciation of the syllable *yah*, in the spirit of the dictum "make a fence around the Torah" (*Avot* 1:1). Less frequently, the tetragrammaton is marked to indicate its pronunciation as Elohim.
6. Moore, "Notes on the Name," 35.
7. Wilkinson, *Tetragrammaton*, 212.
8. Exod 14:19–21.
9. Jer 25:26, 51:41.

10. Jer 51:1.
11. With the final letter *heh*, (making it *yod, dalet, yod, dalet, yod, heh*) it spells "God's Friend."
12. Sameth, "Is God Transgender?"

Chapter 1

13. *Elohim nitzav ba'adat el*, "God stands in the divine council," *b'kerev elohim yishpot*, "in the midst of the gods He passes judgment." Psalm 82:1. See Morgenstern, "Mythological Background of Psalm 82," 29–98.
14. Evidence that at least some Israelites believed that YHWH had a female consort, a goddess named Asherah, suggests that, in popular belief, YHWH was male. Israelites who believed YHWH was male and Asherah was his female consort can be understood as followers of an Israelite "popular religion." The biblical authors railed against the worship of Asherah as proponents of an Israelite "official religion," and the priestly scribes—who knew the secret that YHWH was dual gendered—acted as keepers of an Israelite "elite religion." Although Asherah is a goddess in the Sumerian and Ugaritic pantheons, in the Hebrew Bible, "asherah" seems in most instances to refer not to the goddess herself but to a cultic object associated with her: perhaps a living or stylized tree (symbolizing, perhaps, the tree of life) or a pole (perhaps a stylized phallus intended to attract her attention). For more on Asherah, see Hadley, *Cult of Asherah*, 57. For more on Asherah worship as an Israelite folk religion, see Dever, *Did God Have a Wife?* On the discovery in 1975–1976 at Kuntillet Ajrud in the Sinai Desert of pottery on which was inscribed "I bless you by our guardian YHWH and by his Asherah," see Meshel, "Did Yahweh Have a Consort?" 24–34. In the Hebrew Bible, Asherah worship is said to have been practiced by Maacah, mother of Judah's King Asa (1 Kings 15:1–14, 2 Chr 11:20–22, 2 Chr 15:16) and was understood to have been ignominiously introduced to Israel by Queen Jezebel, wife of King Ahab (1 Kings 16:33, 18:19). 2 Kings 21:7 depicts the unfaithful King Manasseh setting up a *pesel ha'Asherah*, a graven image of Asherah in the Temple.
15. Durant, *Story of Civilization*, 242.
16. Harper, *Assyrian and Babylonian Literature*, 438–39.
17. Frymer-Kenksy, *In the Wake of the Goddesses*, 25–30.
18. Dorman, *Akhenaten*.
19. We will later see this in a line from Deut (6:4), a line known to Jews as the Shema, which declares that the deity worshiped by southern Israelites, YHWH, and the deity worshiped by northern Israelites, El, are one.
20. *Enuma Elish*'s answer is that the world had been created from the mating of a primordial being, Apsu, personifying the sweet underground waters,

with a primordial being, Tiamat, personifying the salty oceanic waters. See King, *Seven Tablets of Creation*, lines 1–9, p. 77.

21. A number of different versions were memorialized on the pyramid walls. They have in common with each other a primordial oceanic chaos—personified by the primordial Nu—out of which dry land, the foundation of the world, eventually emerges and separates. See Allen, *Ancient Egyptian*, 9, 273, 305n55, 427.

22. In the second millennium BCE, Mesopotamia was bicultural and bilingual. And "bi-lingual" doesn't quite capture how profoundly intertwined the languages became. Linguists refer to Akkadia-Sumeria as a *sprachbund*, a place of truly deep linguistic convergence, where speakers of Sumerian (an isolate language) and Akkadian (a Semitic language) not only spoke but also shaped each other's language.

23. "The speech of mankind is truly one." "Enmerkar," Electronic Text Corpus.

24. The invention of writing is said to have independently been created at least three times—in the Middle East as early perhaps as 3400 BCE and later in China and the Mayan Empire.

25. Scholars use the terms *therianthropy* to refer to the combining of animal and human forms and *theriocephaly* to specifically refer to the combining of a human body with an animal head.

26. We're left to wonder how to interpret bird-man and bison-man. The French archaeologist and anthropologist André Leroi-Gourhan saw the cave symbols as depicting the interplay between male and female, which he believed to be the great universal trope. A pioneer in the study and interpretation of Paleolithic cave art, Leroi-Gourhan devised an intricate and overarching interpretative system to account for every one of the forms found depicted on the walls of the caves at Lascaux and elsewhere. See Leroi-Gourhan, *Dawn of European Art*. See also Conkey, "Interpretation of European 'Paleolithic Art,'" 298, 300–302. See also *Archaeology*, Thomas and Kelly, 305. More recent scholars have submitted Leroi-Gourhan's theory to close scrutiny and have cast doubt on many of the particulars. See Gombrich, "Miracle at Chauvet." But Leroi-Gourhan was certainly on to something. He was influenced by one of the fathers of modern anthropology, Claude Lévi-Strauss, and by a founder of the school of structural linguistics, Ferdinand de Saussure. In his *The Raw and the Cooked*, Lévi-Strauss argues that a universal code is present in all myth. Drawing not only on de Saussure's linguistic theory of structuralism but also on Hegel's idea of thesis, antithesis, and synthesis, Lévi-Strauss argues that a code of binary oppositions—"the raw and the cooked, the fresh and the decayed, the moistened and the burned, etc."—is the fundamental pivot around which a culture's entire project of finding true meaning turns. See Lévi-Strauss, *The Raw and the Cooked*, 1.

Chapter 2

27. The Hebrew *omayn* (Num 11:12) was translated as "nursing-father" by the Jewish Publication Society (1917). The same translation is to be found in the earlier King James Bible (1611). This is supported by the first-ever translation of the Torah into Greek, the Septuagint (third century BCE), which rendered the word *tithenos*, Greek for "nurse." (See Peter W. Flint's translation of Numbers in Pietersma, *English Translation of the Septuagint*.) Moreover, the context makes clear that the meaning "wet nurse" is intended, as the verse describes Israel as *ha'yonayk*, "the suckling child." The nursing-father trope continues in Deuteronomy. There, God, called "Father" (Deut 32:6), is said to have suffered labor pains (*m'chol'lecha*) in Deut 32:18 and given birth to (*y'lad'cha*) and suckled (*va'yayni'kay'hu*) Israel in Deut 32:6, 18, 13. The trope continues in the Talmud. There, Rabbi Yosef and Abayye debate the meaning of a miracle said to have been performed for a man whose wife died leaving a nursing child, whereupon the man's breasts opened, allowing him to nurse the child himself. Rabbi Yosef said the miracle was performed on account of the man's greatness; Abbaye said the miracle proved how lowly the man was, that nature had to be changed for him. (Babylonian Talmud, Shabbat 53b.)

28. Redford, *Egypt, Canaan, and Israel*, 273 (cited in Wright, *Evolution of God*, 501n60. Wright also cites Cross, *Canaanite Myth*, 61–62, who says the southern Palestinian lists featuring the name are from the fourteenth and thirteenth century BCE, Rainey, "Israel in Merenptah's Inscriptions," 57–75, and Dever, *Who Were the Israelites*, 150–51).

29. The same reference appears in a list at the later-built Amarah-West of Rameses II, about 50 kilometers north of Soleb, also in Sudan.

30. Redford, *Egypt, Canaan, and Israel*, 271–73.

31. Rainey, "Israel in Merenptah's Inscription," 57–75. See also Wright, *Evolution of God*, 114 and 501–2n60 and Dever, *Who Were the Early Israelites?*

32. A survey of the scholarly history on the subject may be found in Van Oorschot and Witte, *Origins of Yahwism*. A critique of a minority view that argues for a northern origin, the so-called Berlin hypothesis, may be found therein, in Leuenberger's "YHWH's Provenance," 157–79.

33. Cross, *Canaanite Myth*, viii.

34. Porten, *Elephantine Papyri*, 146–47, 159, 205, 266. It also appears curiously at times as YHH.

35. Kuenen, *Religion of Israel*, 249.

36. "The physical meaning can hardly be other than *he who causes* rain or lightning to *fall* upon the earth." Smith, *Old Testament*, 423; Wellhausen, *Israelitische*, 11.

37. Lieber, *Etz Hayim*, 330. YHWH is translated as "The Eternal" in Plaut and

Stein, *The Torah*. A history of this interpretation can be found in Wilkinson, *Tetragrammton*, 1–41 (see especially pp. 2–3n6).

38. Other examples of the Hebrew Bible's folk etymologies include: "The man named his wife Eve because [she] was the mother of all the living" (Gen 3:20); "Therefore it was called Babel, because there YHWH confused the language of all the earth" (Gen 11:9); "And therefore that place was called Beer-sheba, for there the two of them swore an oath" (Gen 21:31); "And Abraham called the place *Adonai-yireh,* therefore the saying 'On the mountain of YHWH there is vision'" (Gen 22:14); "The first one came out red, like a hairy mantle, and so they called his name Esau. Then his brother came out, in his hand he held Esau's heel, so they called his name Jacob" (Gen 25:25–26); "He called that well Esek, because they contended with him" (Gen 26:20); "And he said 'Your name shall no longer be called Jacob, but Israel, because you have striven with beings divine and human and have prevailed'" (Gen 32:29); "And Jacob called the place Peniel, for I have seen God face to face yet my life has been preserved" (Gen 32:31); "She called his name Moses, saying 'Because from the water I drew him'" (Exod 2:10); "And they came to Marah, and they could not drink the water of Marah because it was bitter, therefore its name was called Marah" (Exod 15:23); "The name of the place was called Massah and Meribah, because the Children of Israel quarreled, and because they tried YHWH" (Exod 17:7); and "And the name of the place was called Taberah, because a fire of YHWH had broken out against them" (Num 11:3). See as well the folk etymologies of the children of Jacob, Rachel, Leah, Bilhah, and Zilpah (Gen 29:31–30:24, 35:18).

39. Brettler, "Kabbalat Shabbat," 24.
40. Diamond, *Guns, Germs, and Steel,* 232–33.
41. Murray, "The Name of Ra," 80–86.
42. Parke-Taylor, *Yahweh,* 4.
43. Rav Ze'ev Wolf of Zhitomer, a student of the Maggid of Mezritch, in *Or Ha'Meir,* a commentary to the Torah portion *Va-yehi* (Gen 49:1). See Green, *Speaking Torah,* 162; Hebrew pp. 424–26.
44. Hoffman, *In the Beginning,* 20–21.
45. Hoffman, 28, 31–34.
46. Hoffman, 31–34.
47. "As early as the 12th century, certain Jewish philosophers, specifically Jehuda Halevi and Abraham ibn Ezra, made certain observations about the fact that the four consonants which are found in the two most important divine names in the Torah—the name *Jahwe* and the name *Ehjeh*—are precisely those which are also used as vowel letters in Hebrew, *matres lectionis*. They represent, as it were, a connection between consonants and vowels, and one could regard them as the spiritual elements among the

consonants. According to the philosophers this made them particularly suited as practical symbols of the divine spirit in the heavenly body, and thus suited to be the elements forming those two divine names." Scholem, "Name of God," 172.

48. This type of writing is called *boustrophedon*, meaning "as the ox plows."
49. Israel Museum, "Priestly Benediction."
50. Israel Museum, "Hebrew letter."
51. Israel Museum, "Hebrew letter (ostracon)."
52. Louvre, "The Mesha Stele."
53. The name Elijah—in Hebrew, *Eliyahu*—is particularly striking. If we take *yah* as a reverse-spelling cryptogram for the Hebrew pronoun *hi*, meaning "she," Elijah—who was in later rabbinic lore the herald of the Messiah—can be read as a crypto name meaning "My God [*Eli*] He [*Hu*] is She [*Yah*]."
54. Substitution had been taken to a literal extreme in Mesopotamia. In ancient Hittite and Mesopotamian literature, the *šar pūhī* ("substitute king") ritual is described. In this ritual, the true king would be hidden and a substitute king would be placed on the throne, with the true king being restored to the throne with only the passing of whatever perceived danger had triggered the substitution. The ritual was practiced, for instance, during a solar or lunar eclipse. It may sound glamorous, but the part of the substitute king was not a role one wanted to land. The literature goes on to describe how the substitute king, "having ruled his predetermined period, is put to death, after which the king re-ascends his throne as if nothing had happened." Wright, *Disposal of Impurity*, 22. Whether a connection exists between the ritual of the substitute king and the use of a substitute name for God, it beggars belief that the ancient Israelite priests might ever have shared the name of God with commoners.
55. In Sarai's case, the letter *yod* drops out. The Talmud (Jerusalem, Sanhedrin 2:6) explains that the *yod* taken from Sarai's name was divided into two *heh*s, one of which was added to Abram's name and the other to Sarai's name.

Chapter 3

56. 2 Kings 22:3–23:27, 23:1–3. (Note that the dating of 628 BCE is based on an alternate account found in 2 Chr 34:3; it places the reforms of Josiah in the twelfth year of his reign rather than his eighteenth. See Tadmor, "Period of the First Temple," 149); 2 Kings 23:3. The term used, va'yichrot, literally "he cut," is the technical term used to describe establishing or solemnizing a covenant.
57. 2 Kings 22:8, 23:2.

58. The found book forbade the worship of other gods (2 Kings 23:4), countryside altars (2 Kings 23:5, 8), temple prostitutes (2 Kings 23:7), and household gods and idols (2 Kings 23:24), and it established (or, as the Book of Kings has it, reestablished) the observance of the festival of Passover (2 Kings 23:21–23).
59. See Seltzer, *Jewish People*, 31–32.
60. The first exiles left Jerusalem ca. 598 BCE. The first returnees entered Jerusalem ca. 538 BCE, sixty years later.
61. See Friedman, *Who Wrote the Bible?*, 232.
62. Babylonian Talmud, Sukkah 20a; Babylonian Talmud, Sanhedrin 21b. "When afterwards it was again forgotten, Hillel the Babylonian came up from Babylon and restored it again; and when it was again forgotten, R. Chiyya and his children came and restored it again." Babylonian Talmud, Sukkah 20a.
63. Babylonian Talmud, Sanhedrin 21b.
64. Ezra knew the secret pronunciation of its "proper sounds," Babylonian Talmud, Yoma 69b.
65. This tradition is said to have been taught by Rabbi Yosef in the name of Rav, Babylonian Talmud, Yoma 69b.
66. The Second Temple was completed and dedicated around the year 516 BCE.
67. Regarding patriarchy's "inextricable linkage to militarism," see Lerner, *Creation of Patriarchy*, 228–29.
68. "Man O'War," *Ish Milchamah*, Exod 15:3. See as well Deut 32:41. The reference there to God's *barak harbi*—"lightning (swift) sword"—was the inspiration for the "terrible swift sword" in the song "The Battle Hymn of the Republic." Man O' War should more properly be translated as "War Partner."
69. Matt 10:34 (New Kings James Version).
70. Qur'an, Sura 9:5, and other so-called sword verses.
71. Eve is referred to as "he" (*heh, vov, alef*, Gen 3:12). According to the Masoretic tradition, the masculine pronoun in Gen 3:12 is vowelized *hi* (she). Francis Brown, S. R. Driver, and Charles A. Briggs note that *heh, vov, alef* vowelized *hi* (and *heh, yod, alef* vowelized *hu*) occurs in only a handful of occasions outside the Pentateuch (1 Kings 17:15, Isa 30:33, Job 31:11, Psalm 73:16, Eccl 5:8, 1 Chr 29:16), "prob[ably] for the sake of removing gramm[atical] anomalies . . . The origin of the peculiarity in the Pent[ateuch] is uncertain. It can hardly be a real archaism: for the fact that Arab., Aram, and Eth. have distinct forms for masc[uline] & fem[inine] shows that both must have formed part of the original Semitic stock, and consequently of Hebrew as well, from its earliest

existence as an independent language" (Brown et al., *Hebrew and English Lexicon*, 215). A story which purports to tell how a disagreement over whether to scribe *heh, vov, alef* or *heh, yod, alef* in a number of places in the Torah was resolved appears in Soferim 6,4. The story, which dates perhaps to the Second Temple period, recounts an incident which may never have occurred. Rather, it may have been intended to memorialize a grammatical oddity in the text—that in the Pentateuch she (*hi*) appears as heh—yod—alef only eleven times—thereby putting future scribes on notice that they are not to "correct" the Pentateuch's many heh—vov—alef "mistakes." Highly noteworthy are Gen 38:25, and Num 5:13 and 5:14 in each of which *hi* (she) is spelled both heh—vov—alef and heh—yod—alef. Most noteworthy is Gen 20:5, in which *hi* spelled heh—vov—alef and *hi* spelled heh—yod—alef appear back to back. Another version of the Soferim story appears in the Jerusalem Talmud, Ta'anit 20b. Similar to the Ta'anit version is the account in Sifre Deuteronomy, Zot ha'Bracha, chap. 33, para. 356.

Noah repairs to "her tent" (Gen 9:21). The word *alef, heh, lamed, heh* in this verse is, according to Masoretic tradition, publicly pronounced *ohalo* (meaning "his tent") as if spelled *alef, heh, lamed, vov*. The final *heh* as masculine possessive may well be an archaic spelling. In that case, *heh* would not have been treated as a vowel but rather a true consonant. We see this form in connection with other males in the Torah (e.g., Abram at Gen 12:8, 13:3; and Israel at Gen 35:21). But we know that in time, the normative spelling changed to *alef, heh, lamed, vov*. Moreover, the redactor knows of this "modern" spelling (with the unambiguously masculine suffix letter *vov*) because the redactor uses it (for instance at Gen 26:25, Exod 33:8, Lev 14:8, and Num 11:10). Whatever reasons may be cited for old and new forms and spellings occurring side by side in the Hebrew Bible, the gender-bending under consideration here is jarring to the point that its intentionality can be all but assumed. The spelling is too suggestive of the feminine and would have been to the readers of the redactor's text.

Rebecca is referred to as a "young man" (*nun, ayin, resh*, Gen 24:14, 16, 28, 55, 57). In the Torah, this word can be vocalized either as *na'ar*, meaning "young man," or *na'arah*, meaning "young woman." But use of this assumedly archaic spelling in the Torah seems to have been intended to create grammatical gender ambiguity. Because the Hebrew language at first had no way to indicate vowels, in very ancient times "young man" and "young woman," although pronounced differently, would have been spelled the same—*nun, ayin, resh*. But later the "helper" letter *heh* (a consonant doubling as the vowel "a") was added to the end of the word for "young woman" to help facilitate its pronunciation. *Nun, ayin, resh, heh* then became the standard spelling for "young woman." Except in the Torah, throughout the entire Hebrew Bible, in every text in which the word "young woman" appears, the word is spelled with the helper letter *heh* (notably including Amos 2:7; the text of Amos, in the main, is arguably as old as its eighth century BCE setting). Helper letters are referred to by grammarians as *matres lectionis*, "mothers of reading." We see the helper letter *heh* used throughout the Torah to distinguish the feminine form from the masculine (sometimes called "unmarked") form. That's why in the Torah Joseph is a *yeled* ("boy," Gen 37:30), but Dinah is a *yaldah* ("girl," Gen 34:4). Moses is a *navi* ("prophet," Deut 34:10), but Miriam is a *n'vi'ah* ("prophetess," Exod 15:20). Noah's eldest son Shem is *ha'gadol* ("the elder," Gen 10:21), but Laban's eldest daughter Leah is *ha'g'dolah* ("the elder," Gen 29:16). Noah's young son Ham is *ha'katan* ("the young," Gen 9:24), but Laban's young daughter Rachel is *ha'k'tanah* ("the young," Gen 29:16). Each of the feminine-marked words above is spelled with the final helper letter *heh*. Given all that, we might expect to find the word "young woman" also spelled with a *heh*. But with one exception in the Torah, it is not. In the Torah, the word "young woman," pronounced *na'arah*, is spelled without the *heh* more than twenty times (see the references to Dinah at Gen 34:3, 34:12). Spelled without *heh*, the word appears repeatedly in a short section of Deut (22:15–29). Curiously, this instance is in the middle of a dense cluster that has the Torah's one-time-only appearance of the word spelled with the helper letter *heh* (Deut 22:19). Actually, this placement is more than curious. It is as if we had been reading an Old English text in which the word "erst" (Old English for "first") repeated over and over, and then all of a sudden the word "first" popped up. Various reasons may account for spelling differences in the Torah. In this case, we can reasonably conclude that the redactor made an intentional decision to spell "young woman" the old-fashioned, archaic, grammatically gender-ambiguous way (meaning, without the helper letter *heh*), long after the spelling of that word had presumably changed, so that the word would appear as if "young man." The public reader would been instructed to pronounce the word as *na'arah*, "young woman." So those who heard the Torah being read out loud would have been unaware of the scribal tradition. But the unnecessary grammatical gender-ambiguity in the text was a signal to those in the know of the closely held priestly scribal tradition concerning gender fluidity, both human and divine.

Adam is referred to as "them" (*otam*, Gen 1:27). It may be argued that the word *adam* is used here to mean "humankind" and that such a collective noun can be treated either as singular or plural (e.g., "army"). But Gen 1:27 refers to Adam both as "it" (*oto,* singular) and "them" (*otam*, plural) in the same sentence. Moreover, Adam's having been created "male and female" "in the image of God" was taken to mean by the rabbis that Adam was created as an intersex being—singular in one respect, plural in another. Exactly how Adam was constituted as an intersex being was debated. Rabbi Jeremiah ben Elazar held that Adam was an androgyne, while Rabbi Samuel bar Nachman held that Adam was more like conjoined male-female twins. (See *Bereishit Rabbah* 8:1.)

ENDNOTES

Mordechai is said to have been Esther's "nursing-father" (*ohmen,* Esther 2:7). It may be argued that the word *ohmen* would be better translated as "foster father" or "supporter" and that another word in Hebrew, *meneqet,* means "wet nurse." But just as in English it is more common to say that a mother is "nursing" than to say that she is "suckling" even though the latter is more specific, so too in Hebrew the words *ohmenet* ("nurse") and *meneqet* ("one who suckles") can be used interchangeably. Just as in English one can "nurse" a baby or "nurse" a wound, so too in the Hebrew Bible the Hebrew word for "nurse" is found in reference to babies (Ruth 4:16) and wounds (Prov 27:6). The grammatically masculine form of the word *ohmen* is admittedly strange. But the Septuagint (the earliest translation of the Five Books of Moses) renders it as *tithenos*—Greek for "nurse" (Num 11:12; see Peter W. Flint's translation of Numbers in Pietersma, *New English Translation of the Septuagint*). Although translating *ohmen* as "foster father" or "supporter" is certainly possible, if we were to do so in every instance, we would miss an important hallmark of the Hebrew Bible: wordplay. An example is the above cited Prov 27:6: "The wounds [inflicted by] a friend are nursing."

The future kings of Israel are prophesied to be nursing kings (*m'lachim omnayich,* Isa 49:23). As with the Esther verse, it may be argued that *omnayich* here means that the future kings will be "your supporters." But the verse goes on, "their noble-women your suckling ones (*maynikotaich*)." The parallelism allows that *omnayich* and *maynikotaich* in this verse may be intended as synonyms. In that case, the future kings will not be supporting but rather breast-feeding their subjects. That this is the correct reading seems confirmed by Isa 60:16, which states explicitly, "Kings' breasts shall you suck [*tinaki*]." Another instance of the nursing king/nursing father trope appears at Num 11:12. This is the passage in which Moses complains to God that he, Moses, is in effect not woman enough for the task God has put before him: "Did I conceive (*ha'riti*) this people? Did I give birth to them (*y'lid'tihu*) that You should say to me: Carry them in your bosom as the nursing-father (*ha'ohmen*) carries the suckling infant (*ha'yonayk*)?" Both Isaac Leeser and Abraham Benisch— the first Jews to translate the Five Books of Moses into English (1845 and 1851, respectively)—rendered *ohmen* here as "nursing-father," as had the earlier King James Bible. The verse inspired G. F. Handel's 1727 coronation anthem, written for Queen Caroline, "Kings shall be thy nursing fathers" (Handel, "Kings Shall Be Thy Nursing Fathers," from *My Heart Is Inditing, Coronation Anthem No. 4,* HWV, 261).

God is addressed both in the second-person singular masculine and the second-person singular feminine. The second-person singular masculine (*attah*) is first used, by Hagar addressing God, in Gen 16:13. The second-person singular feminine (*at*) is used by Moses addressing God in Num 11:15. Rashi attempts to explain this by saying that Moses had grown weak (presumably Rashi meant that when Moses got too weak to pronounce *attah*, he broke off after the first syllable). Ehrlich assumes *at* to be the archaic form of *attah* (before the advent of *matres lectionis*). See Milgrom, *JPS Torah Commentary*, 86n31. Assuming *at* to be the archaic form of *attah*, the question arises: Why in this one instance would the redactor not have brought the spelling up to date, choosing instead to preserve the gender-ambiguous form?

God your Father (*avicha*, Deut 32:6) endures convulsions of labor (*m'chol'lecha*, Deut 32:18), gives birth (*y'lad'cha*, Deut 32:18), and suckles (*va'yayni'kay'hu*, Deut 32:13).

72. The fish is male (*dag*) in Jonah 2:1 and female (*daga*) in Jonah 2:2. The Hebrew text does not refer to the animal as a whale. The writers of the *midrash* struggled to rationalize the male vs. female fish discrepancy: "Jonah was so comfortable in the [male] fish that he felt no need to pray for deliverance; hence God sent another fish—this time a female with 365 small fish already in its belly—and Jonah was transferred there." Plaut, *Haftarah Commentary*, 657n20. In his retelling, Louis Ginzberg cites *Bet ha-Midrasch* I, 96–105, in *Midrash Jonah*, and states that "only this source [*Midrash Jonah*] contains the episode with the female fish." Ginzberg, *Legends of the Jews*, vol. 6, 350n31.

73. Pietersma, *English Translation of the Septuagint*, 751.

74. Kugel, *Bible As It Was*, 18, 405–6. See as well Hellner-Eshed, *River Flows From Eden*, 365–78.

75. Ben Sira quoted in the Babylonian Talmud, Hagigah 13a. See also *Bereishit Rabbah* 8:3.

76. The expression *v'som sechel* in Neh 8:8 has presented a challenge to translators. The word implies twisting and turning. The shepherds did not *hiscilu*, and so their flock was scattered (Jer 11:21). The patriarch Israel is said to *sicayl* his arms when he placed his right hand to the left and his left hand to the right (Gen 48:14). The word can be used in a positive sense—wise, capable, successful, or prosperous—or in a negative sense—bereaved, childless, stumbling, or folly. In the context of Neh 8:8, it reflects the idea, according to Hindy Najmin, that "the Torah cannot simply be read and understood in a straightforward way." Najman, "Nehemiah," 1700.

77. This tradition was codified by the scholar-scribes known as the Masoretes ("Tradition Keepers"). A book with these agreed-upon "corrections" (called a *Tikkun* or "Corrected" text) can be found to this day in every synagogue, used as an aid by the public readers. Some "mistakes" are so obvious and so regularly occurring that the Masoretes did not even feel the need to make a note in the margin of the Corrected text. A case like this is called a *qere perpetuum*, or "perpetual (correction to) reading." The public reader's out-loud correction of a "wrongly" gendered pronoun in the Torah is considered a *qere perpetuum*, "a perpetual convention of reading." A number of theories about the origin of the *qere* and *ketiv*

system have been advanced. No one theory is sufficient to explain every instance of its occurrence. Rabbi Don Isaac Abravanel (fifteenth century) suggested that at least in some cases the system was intended to convey "mysteries" of the Torah. (See Graves, and Leiman, 416–72.)

78. Van der Toorn, *Scribal Culture*, 106 (emphasis mine).
79. The late literary theorist Roland Barthes suggested a reading strategy that he called *proairetism*—a way of reading that focuses attention on the play of names in a text. See Barthes, *S/Z*, 83.
80. Gen 32:29 and 35:10; Gen 32:30 and 35:14.
81. Gen 41:45.
82. Gen 12:1, 12:5.
83. Gen 28:11.
84. Gen 35:7.
85. Exod 2:1.
86. Exod 6:20.
87. Exod 2:4; 2:7–8.
88. Exod 15:20. In fact, she is identified as Aaron's sister. That makes her Moses's sister because Aaron and Moses are brothers. But Miriam is referred to by name as Moses's sister in only the Torah's very last mention of her, Num 26:59.
89. Exod 2:16.
90. Exod 2:18.
91. Exod 3:1, 4:18, Num 10:29.
92. Gen 7:7, 13, 16, 18.
93. Gen 37:35.
94. Gen 32:30.
95. Exod 2:5–10.
96. Gen 15:2.
97. Servant (Gen 24:2–17); man (Gen 24:21–32); servant (Gen 24:34–53); man and servant (Gen 24:61).
98. Laban called it *Yegar-sahadutha*, while Jacob called it *Gal-ed*; Jacob also called it *Mizpah* (Gen 31:47; 49).
99. Horeb (Exod 3:1, 17:6); "Mount Sinai" again, in the Torah's final reference (Deut 33:2). This seems to leave open the possibility that the place name is Horeb, and that it is mostly referred to in the Torah as "[the unnamed] Mountain [of the] Sinai [desert]."
100. Gen 35:18.

ENDNOTES

101. Gen 5:32, 6:10, 7:13, 9:18, 10:1, 10:2, 10:6, 10:21.

102. Num 20:22–29. The Masoretic text vocalizes the name as *Hor;* but unvocalized, the name is most obviously *Har,* "mountain."

103. Other examples include:
    The opening line of the Book of Leviticus, "And he called to Moses," does not provide the name of the speaker. Then the Torah reveals that the speaker is God. Why not just say "And God called to Moses"? Why the convoluted construction?

    Place names are also changed more than once: Jacob changes the name of Luz to Beth El three different times (Gen 28:19, 35:7, 35:15).

    A man named Zohar, a son of Simeon, later appears as Zerach and a man named Job, a son of Issachar, later appears as Jashub ("Zohar," Gen 46:10; "Zerach," Num 26:13; "Job," Gen 46:13; "Jashub," Num 26:24).

    Esau marries Judith, the daughter of Beeri the Hittite, and Basemath, the daughter of Elon the Hittite (Gen 26:34). They later appear as Adah, daughter of Elon the Hittite, and Oholibamah, daughter of Anah, daughter of Zibeon the Hivite (Gen 36:2). Rashi, in his commentary on the Torah, says these names are different for the same people—that Adah is Basemath and Oholibamah is Judith. Moreover, as Rashi points out in his comment to Gen 36:2, Anah is Zibeon's son, not his daughter, per Gen 36:24. A third wife appears, Basemath, daughter of Ishmael (Gen 36:3), whom Rashi points out had been identified (in Gen 28:9) as Mahalath, daughter of Ishmael.

    Another oddity is that the name Israel is, in Hebrew, made up exclusively of the first letters of the names of the matriarchs and patriarchs: *yod* for Yitzchock (Isaac), Yisrael (Israel), and Ya'akov (Jacob); *shin* for Sarah; *resh* for Rachel and Rivka (Rebecca); *alef* for Avraham (Abraham); *lamed* for Leah. The name Israel is widely accepted to mean "he strives with God." But, as Nahum Sarna points out, "The precise meaning of this name is impeded by many difficulties. . . . [I]n names formed by a verb combined with '*el,* the divine element is usually the subject of the action, not its indirect object. *Yisra'el,* therefore, should properly mean 'God strives,' not 'He strives with God.' None of the suggestions proposed to explain the verbal element has yielded satisfaction. Until more philological evidence is forthcoming, the true explanation escapes us." Sarna, "Excursus 25," 404–5.

    What is the significance of Moses's changing Hosea's, son of Nun, name to Joshua? (Num 13:16). No reason is given.

    According to Genesis, in the third generation of humankind, during the time of Enosh, people began to invoke the name YHWH (Gen 4:26). Abram, Isaac, and Jacob all invoked the name. How, then, could God later say to Moses, "I did not make myself known [to Abraham, Isaac, and Jacob] by my name YHWH?" (Exod 6:3).

104. The hypothesis was revised many times over the years to include more

than four sources: J1, J2, J3, E1, E2, L, K, S, N, Pa, Pb, and more. See Blenkinsopp, *Pentateuch*, 14.

105. Blenkinsopp, *Pentateuch*, 19–25.
106. Cassuto originally published *Torath HaTeudoth* in Hebrew in 1941; an English translation, *The Documentary Hypothesis and the Composition of the Pentateuch: Eight Lectures by Umberto Cassuto*, first appeared in 1961.
107. Whybray, *Making of the Pentateuch*, 19.
108. Alter, *Art of Biblical Narrative*, 138.
109. Alter, *Art of Biblical Narrative*, 133.
110. Babylonian Talmud, Bava Batra 15a; and Ibn Ezra on Gen 12:6.
111. Wellhausen had a notorious "aversion to Judaism." See Blenkinsopp, *Pentateuch*, 8, 12.
112. Joyce, *Ulysses*, 754.
113. I do not mean to imply that Joyce's novel doesn't have any textual errors. But a "corrected" version by Hans Walter Gabler (1984) was so controversial that it had to be withdrawn. Without doubt, some copyist errors exist in the Torah.
114. Gen 1:26, 27.
115. *Bereishit Rabbah* 8:1. Friedman and Simon, *Midrash Rabbah*, 54.
116. *Bereishit Rabbah* 8:1.
117. Horowitz, "Image of God in Man," 185.
118. Plato, *Cratylus* 402a.
119. Hippolytus, *Refutations* 9.10.3.
120. The brief period of autonomy, the period of Hasmonean independence, lasted a little more than a century, beginning about 160 BCE.
121. Mishnah, *Sotah*, 7:6.
122. See as well Babylonian Talmud, *Kiddushin* 71a.

Chapter 4

123. The Jerusalem (a.k.a. Palestinian) Talmud was finalized, mostly in Tiberias, in the latter half of the fourth century. The larger and ultimately much more influential Babylonian Talmud was finalized in Sura in the fifth century. Safrai, "Era of the Mishnah," 355, 379.
124. *Daily Prayer Book*, 115–16.
125. The story of the tragic fate of Rabbi Chanina ben Teradyon, who pronounced THE NAME publicly, "according to its letters," appears in the Babylonian Talmud, Avodah Zarah, 17b–18a.

126. According to Josephus, his name was Marcus Antonius Julianus. Josephus, *Wars of the Jews or History of the Destruction of Jerusalem*, book 6, chap. 4, section 3.

127. The makeup of the Sanhedrin during the time of the Temple is not entirely clear. Jewish sources represent the Sanhedrin as being led by scholars—a *nasi* and an *av bet din*. Hellenistic sources suggest the head of the Sanhedrin to have been the high priest or king. See Mantel, "Sanhedrin," 837.

128. Babylonian Talmud, Kiddushin 71a.

129. Babylonian Talmud, Sanhedrin 95a. In time, such miracle stories involving THE NAME would become increasingly popular. Another story has it that the Egyptian man the Torah describes beating a Hebrew man (Exod 2:1) died when Moses did no more than utter THE NAME. This rabbinic tale, called a *midrash*, first appears in *Shemot Rabbah* (*Exodus Rabbah*), a work redacted no earlier than the tenth century CE, but draws on much older material. The story became widely known when it appeared in the Torah commentary of Rashi. See *Shemot Rabbah* 1:30, available online at Sefaria.org. See Rashi's citation of the work in Rashi, *Chumash with Rashi's Commentary*, 7, 8n14. For the dating of *Shemot Rabbah* (*Exodus Rabbah*), see Herr, "Exodus Rabba," 1067–8.

130. Jerusalem Talmud, Yoma 18b.

131. Jerusalem Talmud, Yoma 18b.

132. Jerusalem Talmud, Yoma 18b.

133. *Sefer Yetizrah* has also been rendered as "The Book of Creation." See Kaplan, *Sefer Yetzirah*, i.

134. Babylonian Talmud, Sanhedrin 65b–67b. In the story on 67b, the work is referred to as *Hilkoth Yetzirah*, "Laws of Creation."

135. "The exact time when the title *gaon* came into use cannot be established. . . . Some hold that this title . . . was not granted until after the Arab conquest of Babylonia (657 CE)." Assaf and Brand, "Gaon," 315.

136. The Greek-influenced Parthian-Iranians ruled to 224 CE, followed by the Sassanian-Iranians to 651 CE, and soon thereafter, the Arabian Muslims.

137. Elbogen, *Jewish Liturgy*, 207.

138. Babylonian Talmud, Hagigah 13a.

139. Babylonian Talmud, Hagigah 11b.

140. Prominent among them were said to have been Rabbi Yochanan ben Zakkai (47 BCE–73 CE), Rabbi Nehunia ben HaKanah (first and second centuries), Rabbi Yehoshua (Joshua) ben Hananiah (d. 131 CE), Rabbi Elazar ben Arach, Rabbi Akiva ben Yosef (ca. 40–ca.137 CE), Rabbi Shimon bar Yochai (first century), and Rabbi Ishmael ben Elisha (90–135 CE). See Kaplan, *Sefer Yetzirah*, xv–xxi.

141. Broome, "Ezekiel's Abnormal Personality," 277–84.

142. Babylonian Talmud, Bava Batra 75b. A close reading of the Ezekiel text seems to hint, as well, at the reverse spelling of THE NAME. According to the school of Chariot mysticism, mystics ascending to God's chariot or throne are called *yordei merkavah*. The term refers not to those who ascend but descend to the chariot. Scholem had termed this reversed direction "an extraordinary expression, whose meaning eludes us (perhaps it means those who reach down into themselves in order to perceive the chariot?)" See Scholem, "Kabbalah," 494. An answer to why the mystics are traveling in reverse may possibly be found in a saying of Ezekiel's younger near contemporary, the Greek mystic philosopher Heraclitus of Ephesus (ca. 535–ca. 475 BCE). He said *Hodos ano kato*, "the path is upward-downward." In the world of the Jewish mystics, reverse directionality can be understood as a hint to the proper (reverse) spelling of THE NAME.

143. Dan 7:9; Babylonian Talmud, Hagigah 14a.

144. Song 1:4.

145. Babylonian Talmud, Yevamot 49b.

146. Babylonian Talmud, Sanhedrin 65b. Given the theme of dual gender, the song sung to Rav Zera at his rabbinic ordination ceremony is noteworthy: "No powder and no paint and no waving [of the hair], and still a graceful gazelle." Babylonian Talmud, Ketuboth, 17a. These words were traditionally sung to a bride.

147. Shaked, Ford, and Bhayro, *Aramaic Bowl Spells*, 100, 243.

148. Origen, *Contra Celsum*, 406.

149. Origen, *Contra Celsum*, 563.

150. In the Five Books of Moses, demons are given scant attention; the word, *shaydim*, appears only in Deuteronomy 32:7.

151. So held the German Jewish scholar Ismar Elbogen. Elbogen, *Jewish Liturgy*, 212.

Chapter 5

152. 1 Maccabees 8:17–20.

153. Scholem, "Ba'al Shem," 5.

154. Halevi uses the plural "Masters of the Names" (*Ba'alei ha-Shemot*), as these masters were known to employ many divine names, not only the tetragrammaton.

155. Halevi, *Kuzari*, 182, 423.

156. For instance, under Saxon law, an adulteress's ears and nose were to be amputated and her husband was permitted to kill her, if he wished.

ENDNOTES

157. Ashtor, "Spain," 225.
158. Kaplan, *The Bahir*, 1.
159. Mommsen, "Petrarch's Conception," 226. See also Nachod, "On His Own Ignorance," 95.
160. Gratian's *Decretum*, the first of six volumes of Canon Law (*Corpus Juris Canonici*) declared that "woman was not made in God's image. . . . It is plain enough from this that wives should be subject to their husbands, and almost be servants." Coulton, *Medieval Panorama*, 272, 383, 615.
161. Sefer ha-Bahir para. 171. Kaplan, *The Bahir*, 65.
162. "The great majority . . . of Jewry as a whole believed . . . the *Zohar* . . . ranked alongside the Bible and the Talmud. . . . Only in modern times, and largely for apologetic reasons, was the Zohar deleted from the canon of what was considered 'mainstream' Judaism." Green, Introduction to *The Zohar*, xxxii. Some rabbis considered the *Zohar* to be Judaism's *most* holy book. "The study of *Sefer ha-Zohar* is higher than any other study." Azulai, *Moreh BeEtzba*, 44.
163. Sefer ha-Bahir, para. 107. Kaplan, *The Bahir*, 40.
164. Sefer ha-Bahir. Kaplan.

"Permission was given that it be permuted and spoken" (para. 111, and Kaplan 42). Rabbi Ahilai's reference is to a twelve-letter name of God, formed by permuting the tetragrammaton three times.

"The Blessed Holy One created Adam male and female . . . because she included both male and female" (para. 198, and Kaplan 80).

"She included both male and female" (para. 198, and Kaplan 80).

"Include male and female" (paras. 83–4, and Kaplan 31). The letters final *nun* and open *mem* are said to contain male and female.

"Remember [zachor] refers to the male [zachar]; keep [shamor] refers to the bride" (para. 182, Kaplan 70).

"The union of masculine and feminine united in the primordial act of creation" (para. 3, Kaplan 1).

The reunion of masculine and feminine (see para. 184, and Kaplan 71).

"It means that it is holy for the Holy Ones [meaning the male and female aspects of God]" (para. 174, Kaplan 67).

"To recognize and know the Unity of Unities, who is unified in all His names" (para. 141, Kaplan 52).

"The soul of the female comes from the Female [aspect of God], and the soul of the male comes from the Male [aspect of God]" (para. 199, Kaplan 80).

165. For more on rabbinic views of Grecian thought, see Babylonian Talmud, Baba Kama 82b–83a.

166. Maimonides, *The Guide*, 80–81.
167. Maimonides, *The Guide*, 89.
168. Maimonides, *The Guide*, 91.
169. Maimonides, *The Guide*, 91.
170. Maimonides, *The Guide*, 251.
171. Maimonides, *The Guide*, 252.
172. Maimonides, *The Guide*, 251.
173. Maimonides, *The Guide*, 216.
174. Maimonides, *The Guide*, 87.
175. Maimonides, *The Guide*, 52.
176. Maimonides, *The Guide*, 251.
177. Maimonides, *The Guide*, 8.
178. Maimonides, *The Guide*, 3.
179. Maimonides, *The Guide*, 3.
180. Maimonides, *The Guide*, 6.
181. Maimonides, *The Guide*, 8.
182. Maimonides, *The Guide*, 94.
183. Maimonides, *The Guide*, 252.
184. Exod 3:14.
185. Maimonides, *The Guide*, 239.
186. Maimonides, *The Guide*, 216.
187. Maimonides, *The Guide*, 216-17.
188. Maimonides, *The Guide*, 218.
189. Maimonides, *The Guide*, 59.
190. "It is probably the major esoteric work least studied in modern scholarship. It is extant in several manuscripts, yet has never been printed and no detailed studies have been dedicated to it." Dan, *Jewish Mysticism*, 129.
191. Scholem, *On the Kabbalah*, 136. Scholem notes, "The text is unprinted. I have used MS Warner 24 in Leiden, in which it appears as an introduction to Eleazar's *Sefer HaShem* (Fol. 237). Bahya ben Asher seems to be referring to it when in 1291, in his Torah commentary (ed. Venice, 1544, 147c) he says on Leviticus 16:30: 'It is a tradition of the mystics to transmit the name of God only over water.'" On the possibility that this was the way of transmission known to Hai Gaon in the eleventh century, see Idel, *Defining Kabbalah*, 101-3.
192. Dan, *Early Kabbalah*, 82.

193. Dan, *Early Kabbalah*, 83.
194. Gen 1:9.
195. Scholem, "Kabbalah," 523.
196. Dan, *Early Kabbalah*, 45.
197. Sefer ha-Bahir, para. 129. Kaplan translates *davek* and *miyuchad* as "attached and unified." Dan has "united and special." See Kaplan, *The Bahir*, 48; Dan, *Early Kabbalah*, 62.
198. Dan, *Early Kabbalah*, 46. Isaac the Blind had also seemed to hint at the need to rearrange these letters when he quotes from the Book of Job: *mi y'shivenu?* "who can turn Him?" Job 23:13, quoted in Dan, *Early Kabbalah*, 73.
199. Dan, *Early Kabbalah*, 43, 55. That God is male and female can also be read as the hidden message of the Explanation of the Four-Lettered Name, in that one of the characters says, "there is no God in the world other than these two!" See also Scholem, "Jacob ben Jacob," 1219.
200. The bestowal of the honorific is attributed to Rabbi Bachya ben Asher. Liebus, "Isaac the Blind," 35.
201. Dan, *Early Kabbalah*, 95–96.
202. Drob, *Doctrine of Coincidentia*, 3.
203. Dan, *Early Kabbalah*, 89–96.
204. Heraclitus, ca. 535–475 BC.
205. "Nicholas nowhere says, in so many words, '*Deus est coincidentia oppositorum*.'" Hopkins, *Nicholas of Cusa*, 7. Still, Nicholas is generally credited with giving the principle its Latin name *coincidentia oppositorum* (*De Docta Ignorantia*, 1440).
206. Scholem translates the expression as "complete indistinguishability of opposites." Scholem, *Kabbalah*, 88.
207. Dan, *Early Kabbalah*, 153, 157.
208. Dan, *Early Kabbalah*, 153, 157.
209. Dan, *Early Kabbalah*, 158.
210. Dan, *Early Kabbalah*, 119.
211. Dan, *Early Kabbalah*, 35.
212. Gottlieb, "Nahmanides," 782.
213. The story appears both in the Babylonian Talmud, Hagigah 14b; and the Jerusalem Talmud, Hagigah 2:1.
214. Dan, *Early Kabbalah*, 154.
215. Dan, *Early Kabbalah*, 174.

ENDNOTES

216. Scholem, "Name of God," 173. Rabbi Jacob ben Sheshet had earlier written about a mystical practice of making the aleph "disappear" when reciting the Shema. "We should quickly pronounce the *alef* so that the mind does not dwell on it for long." Dan, *Early Kabbalah*, 120.

217. Rashi, *Chumash with Rashi's Commentary*, 48n21. To Rashi's point, note the spelling of anachnu ("we") absent the letter alef in Gen 42:11, Ex 16:7–8, and Num 32:32.

218. Isa 41:23, cited by Abulafia in his *Otzar Eden HaGanuz*, Bodleian Library, Oxford, Ms. Or. 606, 160–162. See Kaplan, *Meditation and Kabbalah*, 84–85.

219. Idel, *Kabbalah and Eros*, 44.

220. Gikatilla, *Gates of Light*, 7.

221. Gikatilla, *Gates of Light*, 3, 4.

222. Gikatilla, *Gates of Light*, 6.

223. Matt, *Essential Kabbalah*, 189.

224. The more conventional translation, "I place God before me at all times," cannot be what Gikatilla meant, as it hints at nothing—certainly not "the whole secret."

225. Gikatilla, *Gates of Light*, 5.

226. Gikatilla, *Gates of Light*, 7.

227. Gikatilla, *Gates of Light*, 9.

228. Gikatilla, *Gates of Light*, 9.

229. Gikatilla, *Gates of Light*, 87.

230. Slanders included that Jews desecrated the host and poisoned wells and Jewish men menstruated from the anus. For more on this era, see Schama, *Story of the Jews*, 324–64.

231. The Christian numbering of years had been introduced by a sixth-century monk Dionysius Exiguus (Dennis the Small).

232. "In the older Kabbalah [the] 'neutralization' of all Messianic tendencies, though not complete, was very marked." Scholem, *Major Trends*, 244–45.

233. Maimonides, *Mishneh Torah, Sefer Zemanim, Kiddush ha-Chodesh* (Sanctification of the New Moon) 11:16. He drew on the work of the second-century Rabbi Yose ben Halafta, author of *Seder Olam Rabbah*.

234. Babylonian Talmud, Sanhedrin 97a.

235. Sefer ha-Zohar, para. 1:117a, Matt, *The Zohar*, vol. 1, 180.

236. Sefer ha-Zohar, para. 1:117a, Matt, *The Zohar*, vol. 1, 180.

237. Another reason has been suggested. Aristotelean philosophy was posing a challenge to traditional belief at the time. Moses ben Shem Tov de Leon,

ENDNOTES

in *Midrash ha-Eduth* (1293), writes that revealing the mysteries might allow Jews to understand the deep truths hidden in their scripture, thereby helping "many become wise and retain their faith in God." Scholem, *Major Trends*, 202.

238. A review of scholarship on the question of Zoharic authorship can be found in Fishbane, "The Zohar," 55-58.
239. 2 Sam 13:18.
240. Sameth, "This Dor Swings," 84-91.
241. My understanding is informed by Stein, "The Noun איש ('îš)," 1203-1542, although the conclusion drawn is my own.
242. Sefer ha-Zohar para. 1:18a, Matt, *The Zohar*, vol. 1, 134; the tribe of Joseph is "male," all the other tribes are "female": Sefer ha-Zohar, para. 1:200a, Matt, *The Zohar*, vol. 3, 227; the letter *alef* is male, the letter *bet* female: Sefer ha-Zohar, para. 1:200b, Matt, *The Zohar*, vol. 3, 228. Regarding the letters of THE NAME, Rabbi Abba and Rabbi Shimon bring different teachings. Rabbi Abba held that the letters *yod* and *vav* of THE NAME are masculine, the *he* feminine. Rabbi Shimon held that "all those letters [the *yod*, *he*, and *vav* of THE NAME] are male and female, merging as one in mystery." Sefer ha-Zohar, para. 1:159a, Matt, *The Zohar*, vol. 2, 386.
243. Sefer ha-Zohar, para. 1:232a, Matt, *The Zohar*, vol. 3, 402; Sefer ha-Zohar, para. 1:246a, Matt, *The Zohar*, vol. 3, 506; Sefer ha-Zohar, para. 1:53b, Matt, *The Zohar*, vol. 1, 299.
244. Sefer ha-Zohar, para. 1:159a, Matt, *The Zohar*, vol. 2, page 386; Sefer ha-Zohar para. 1:160a, Matt, *The Zohar*, vol. 2, 394.
245. Sefer ha-Zohar, para. 1:122a, Matt, *The Zohar*, vol. 2, 206.
246. Sefer ha-Zohar, para. 1:182b, Matt, *The Zohar*, vol. 3, 110.
247. Sefer ha-Zohar, para. 1:19a, Matt, *The Zohar*, vol. 1, 144.
248. Sefer ha-Zohar, para. 1:50a, Matt, *The Zohar*, vol. 1, 275.
249. Sefer ha-Zohar, para. 1:85b, Matt, *The Zohar*, vol. 2, 46.
250. Sefer ha-Zohar, para. 1:50a, Matt, *The Zohar*, vol. 1, 275.
251. Sefer ha-Zohar, para. 1:55b, Matt, *The Zohar*, vol. 1, 313-14; Sefer ha-Zohar, para. 1:182b, Matt, *The Zohar*, vol. 3, 109.
252. This is, however, not to suggest an attitude of gender egalitarianism in the Zoharic imagination. Elliot Wolfson has argued that the original dual-gendered human being was understood to have been a "male androgyne." See Wolfson, *Language, Eros, Being* and Wolfson, *Circle in the Square*.
253. Sefer ha-Zohar, para. 1:8a, Matt, *The Zohar*, vol. 1, 51.
254. Sefer ha-Zohar, para. 1:48a, Matt, *The Zohar*, vol. 1, 264.
255. Sefer ha-Zohar, para. 1:148a, Matt, *The Zohar*, vol. 2, 324-25.

256. Sefer ha-Zohar, para. 1:244a, Matt, *The Zohar*, vol. 3, 494.

257. Sefer ha-Zohar, para. 1:132b, Matt, *The Zohar*, vol. 2, 244.

258. Sefer ha-Zohar, para. 1:230a, Matt, *The Zohar*, vol. 3, 386; Sefer ha-Zohar, para. 1:22a, Matt, *The Zohar*, vol. 1, 169–70.

259. The reference is to the first two words of the Torah, both of which begin with the letter *bet*, the second letter of the Hebrew alphabet and the next two words of the Torah, both of which begin with the letter *alef*, the first letter of the Hebrew alphabet. Sefer ha-Zohar, para. 1:2b, Matt, *The Zohar*, vol. 1, 11.

260. Gen 7:23. The word "come" in Hebrew (*bo*) is spelled *bet, alef*—the reverse order of their appearance in the Hebrew alphabet. Sefer ha-Zohar, para. 1:67b, Matt, *The Zohar*, vol. 1, 396.

261. Gen 38:3. The letters of Er's name, *ayin resh*, when reversed as *resh ayin*, spell *ra*, meaning "evil." Sefer ha-Zohar, para. 1:186b, Matt, *The Zohar*, vol. 3, 135.

262. Esau cries, "First he took away my birthright, and now he has taken away my blessing" (Gen 27:36). The letters *chaf* and *resh* in the word *bekhorati*, "my birthright," appear in reverse order, as *resh* and *chaf* in the word *birkhati*, "my blessing." Sefer ha-Zohar, para. 1:145a, Matt, *The Zohar*, vol. 2, 308.

263. Sefer ha-Zohar, para. 1:179a, Matt, *The Zohar*, vol. 3, 83.

264. Sefer ha-Zohar, para. 1:64b, Matt, *The Zohar*, vol. 1, 377.

265. Sefer ha-Zohar, para. 1:202b, Matt, *The Zohar*, vol. 3, 240.

266. Sefer ha-Zohar, para. 1:11b. Matt, *The Zohar*, vol. 1, 78. See also Sefer ha-Zohar, para. 2:100b, 2:257b, 3:74b, 3:127b.

267. Munk, *Torah Commentary*, 209.

Chapter 6

268. Schama, *Story of the Jews*, 365.

269. Schama, *Story of the Jews*, 380, 395.

270. Schama, *Story of the Jews*, 395.

271. Schama, *Story of the Jews*, 384.

272. I am drawing here on Scholem, *Major Trends in Jewish Mysticism*, 247. Moshe Idel questions the adequacy of Scholem's historical approach and "its implicit assumption... that a given cultural and religious phenomenon is closely intertwined with or dependent on its immediate historical predecessors." Idel argues that history "is only one possible path scholars may follow in order to describe the evolution of religious movements; another avenue is phenomenology." See Idel, *Kabbalah: New Perspectives*, 264–65.

ENDNOTES

273. Quoted in Abraham Azulai's introduction to his *Or ha-Hammah* on the Zohar. Scholem, "Kabbalah," 541.
274. Scholem, *Major Trends*, 239.
275. Scholem, *Origins of the Kabbalah*, 298. For more on Kabbalistic views of evil, see Scholem, *Major Trends*, 236, 238, 239.
276. Babylonian Talmud, Shabbat 119a.
277. Maimonides, *The Guide*, 216.
278. De Vidas writes about *yichudim* in his work *Reishit Chokhmah*. See de Vidas, *Beginning of Wisdom*, 39, 42, 89, 240, 298, 310.
279. One type of unification was said to involve uncovering a hidden alignment or state of balance (*mishkal*) between two seemingly unrelated words. The hidden relationship could be uncovered through a process called *gematria*, the calculating of a word's numeric value. Gematria could be done in any number of ways. Simplest was to assign a numeric value to each letter based on its placement in the alphabet (if we were to do this in English, A would equal one, B would equal two). Then another word could be found with the same numeric value, and the hidden relationship between the two words could be brought to light. If we were to do this in English, we might take the words "mercy" and "poor," both of which would have in this schema a numeric value of sixty-four. And then by showing "mercy" to the "poor" we would be doing more than just the right thing; we would, according to Kabbalistic belief, be effecting a divine "unification" (*yichud*), making a repair (*tikkun*) to a breach in the very fabric of reality itself. Another way to make a unification would be to weave or knit holy names together. For example, in English one might begin with the name "LORD." Then one would mentally make a space between each of the letters, creating "L O R D." Then, within the spaces, one would mentally place the letters of the name GOD, creating "L[G]O[O]R[D]D." Finally, one would close the spaces, integrating the two names as one: "LGOORDD." This practice was done in Hebrew, of course, and unifications of this sort could be much more complicated than this. But this essentially is how the practice was done.
280. A complicated Zoharic explanation—that these letter combinations symbolize two different unifications, an "upper" unification and a "lower" one—obscures the plain sense. Based on old Zoharic traditions of male and female letters, a popular explanation was that *YH* and *WH* were both male-female unifications, only at different levels of reality. See Sefer ha-Zohar, para. 1:159a, Matt, *The Zohar*, vol. 3, 386n543.
281. "H'W, this is the Name of the Holy One Blessed Be He." Babylonian Talmud, Shabbat 104a. This comes in the midst of an explication of the meaning of the letters of the Hebrew alphabet, which begins on page 103b. The "short name" (*shem katan*) is explained as forming part of the "great name" (*shem gadol*).

ENDNOTES

282. Wolfson, "Constructions," 19.

283. *Hochmat Avraham Avinu, fols.* 15b–16a, cited in Wolfson, "Constructions," 24.

284. The Ba'al Shem Tov wrote no books. And because so many legends were told about him, little can be said today with any certainty about him as a historical figure. The Ba'al Shem Tov seems to have been born in the Okopy (a fortress town in what was Polish Podolia, today in western Ukraine) in 1698 or 1700; been orphaned at a young age; made his living as a *shochet* (ritual slaughterer); and began expounding his teachings in the *shtetel* town of Medzhybizh (then Poland, today Ukraine) in 1740, where he died in 1760. Recent scholarship has turned up evidence that the Ba'al Shem Tov lived the last twenty years of his life in tax-exempt Jewish community-owned housing, which suggests that his following was much broader than previously believed—not only the poor, common, and uneducated, but the rich, literate, and elite of Medzhybizh seem to have supported his leadership. See Rosman, *Founder of Hasidism*, 166, 177.

285. Aryeh Kaplan, *Meditation*, 215–17.

286. This is according to the Ba'al Shem Tov's contemporary and supporter Rabbi Pinchas of Koretz. See Uffenheimer, *Hasidism as Mysticism*, 233. A third-generation Hasid, Rabbi Menachem Mendel of Vitebsk taught a complicated Lurianic kavvanah for going to the mikvah in the Ba'al Shem Tov's name, but the testimony of Rabbi Pinchas is more reliable. Menachem Mendel left Europe for Sefad in 1777, where the spiritual culture was defined not by the Ba'al Shem Tov but the Ari; and most of the writings we have by Menachem Mendel are from there. For the testimony of Menachem Mendel see Kaplan, *Meditation*, 276–77. For more on Menachem Mendel, see Uffenheimer, 256.

287. Spelled out in full (*heh, vov, alef*). "Look now, for I, I am He." Deut 32:39. See Gikatilla, *Gates of Light*, 358. No doubt this teaching was rooted in the Talmud's declaration that *HW*—which can be vocalized as *Hu* (He)—was a "short name" for God. (Babylonian Talmud, Shabbat 104a.)

288. Spelled out in full (*heh, yod, alef*). *V'hi sh'amdah*, "And She stood for us" from the *Maggid* section of the Passover Haggadah. Rabbi Moses Chaim Ephraim of Sudylkow, *Degel Mahaneh Efrayim*, 45c, quoted in Uffenheimer, *Hasidism as Mysticism*, 313.

289. Other Masters of the Good Name came before him: Elhanan Ba'al Shem Tov; Benjamin Krotoschin Ba'al Shem Tov, Joel Ba'al Shem Tov. Other, earlier *Ba'alei Shem*, Masters of THE NAME, are known to us by name as well: Sekl Loeb Wormser, *Ba'al Shem* of Michelstadt; Selig, the *Ba'al Shem* of Lublin; Chaim Samuel Jacob Falk, the *Ba'al Shem* of London; Wolf, the *Ba'al Shem* of Poland; Rabbi Joel Heilprin, the *Ba'al Shem* of Zamosc (Zamoshtch); Rabbi Joel ben Isaac *Ba'al Shem*; Rabbi Gedaliah, the *Ba'al Shem* of Worms; Eliyahu ben Moshe Loanz, the *Ba'al Shem* of Worms;

Elijah *Ba'al Shem* of Chelm; and the possibly historical, possibly legendary Adam *Ba'al Shem* of Ropshitz. See Scholem, "Ba'al Shem," 7.

290. The term means Pietism but should not be confused with the medieval *Hasidei Ashkenaz*, German Pietists or with the much earlier Second Temple–period *Hasidim ha-Rishonim*, Pietists of Old.

291. A small minority of progressives today can trace their spiritual roots to the Ba'al Shem Tov as well. The progressive movement—"Neo-Hasidim"—was pioneered by Martin Buber and shaped by the late Rabbi Zalman Shachter Shalomi, and Rabbis Arthur Green, Lawrence Kushner, Lynn Gottlieb, Hanna Tiferet Siegel, and Marcia Prager. It is, however, inarguably true that the eighteenth-century European Jewish Orthodox establishment did not see the Hasidim as "conservative." They saw them as a radical threat to the religious order, so much so that social and religious interaction with them was forbidden. The Lithuanian rabbi and leader of European Jewry known as the Vilna Gaon, Rabbi Elijah ben Shlomo Zalman, supported the ban against them, as did his influential disciple Rabbi Chaim of Volozhin. But the Vilna Gaon's opposition had nothing to do with Hasidic belief in God's so-to-speak dual gender. The Vilna Gaon was himself a renowned Kabbalist. He and the Ba'al Shem Tov most certainly held mystical beliefs in common.

292. Green, et al., *Speaking Torah*, 2.

293. The Yemenite-born Kabbalist Shalom Sharabi was at that very moment expanding on Luria's already extensive corpus of kavvanot in Jerusalem.

294. According to the Ba'al Shem Tov's disciple, the Maggid, a student, when studying the words of the Talmudic sage Abbaye, "brings the mind of Abbaye into his body." See Uffenheimer, *Hasidism as Mysticism*, 182.

295. Shuckling is described by Israel Loebel in *Ozer Yisrael* (Shklov 1786), and in *Sefer ha-Vikuah* (Warsaw 1798), cited by Uffenheimer, *Hasidism as Mysticism*, 20.

296. The Ba'al Shem Tov literally says "intercourse with the *Shekhinah*," the feminine "Presence" of God. See Uffenheimer, *Hasidism as Mysticism*, 377n68.

297. *Ahava Raba*, "Great Love," is recited in the morning service. *Ahavat Olam*, "Eternal Love," is recited in the evening service.

298. From *Toldot Ya'akov Yosef*, quoted in Green and Holtz, *Your Word Is Fire*, 73.

299. Buber, *Spirit of the Orient and Judaism*, 76.

300. Sefer ha-Zohar, para. 1:21b–22a, Matt, *The Zohar*, vol. 1, 167–68. "Moses, the man of God; of him and him alone it is said in a striking phrase that he had intercourse with the Shekhinah." Scholem, *Major Trends*, 226.

301. *Union Prayerbook*, 26.

302. Lerner, *Creation of Patriarchy*, 125.//
303. Shapira, *Sacred Fire*, 232.
304. Shapira, *Sacred Fire*, 61.
305. Shapira, *Sacred Fire*, 291.
306. Shapira, *Sacred Fire*, 266. Rabbi Shapira drew this from the last verse of the Kabbalistic hymn *El Mistater* (God of Hiddenness).
307. Shapira, *Sacred Fire*, 221.
308. Shapira, *Sacred Fire*, 61, 222.
309. Polen, *The Holy Fire*, 140. Shaul Magid takes a different view, believing Rabbi Shapira's theological position to have shifted in the wake of the Great Deportation in the summer of 1942. See Magid, "Rebbe of the Warsaw."

Chapter 7

310. Pew, "Religion in Everyday Life."
311. Pew, "'Nones' on the Rise."
312. In Xenophon's *Symposium*, Socrates states that the professional, public reciters of Homer's poems, the rhapsodes, despite knowing the poems by heart, are "stupid" because "they do not know the inner meanings of the poems," the *hyponoiai*. Xenophon, *Memorabilia, Oeconomicus*, 558–61.
313. Importantly, as Benjamin Sammons notes, "allegoresis was not originally conceived of as a mode of interpretation, but rather as a mode of composition attributed to the poets themselves." Sammons, "History and *Hyponoia*," 63.
314. According to a recent survey, 31 percent of Americans believe that God is neither male nor female, 10 percent believe that God is both male and female, and 1 percent believe that God is female. Shannon-Missal, "Americans' Belief."
315. Daly, *Beyond God*, 19.
316. Recent world population studies show slightly more boys and men than girls and women, with the number of people who are transsexual or intersex or who identify as gender-queer, cisgender, bigender, pangender, ambigender, agender, nongendered, intergendered, and gender-fluid currently unknown. "Estimates of the number of transsexuals vary widely, and should be considered anecdotal." Doherty, "The *Trayf* Jew," 13n2.
317. Yeshivat Chovevei Torah, the Jewish "Open Orthodox" seminary; Wijngaard Institute for Catholic Research; Roman Catholic Women Priests; Ordain Women (Mormon); and see Segran, "Rise of the Islamic Feminists," and Silvers and Elewa, "I Am One."

318. The Talmud mentions male (*zachar*), female (*nekevah*), intersex (*androgynos*), indeterminate (*tumtum*), female to male (*ay'lonit*) and male to female (*saris*).

319. Killermann, *Guide to Gender*, 81–88.

320. "An estimated one in every two thousand newborn babies, according to the American Medical Association, is born with initially ambiguous genitalia." Browning, *Fate of Gender*, 225.

321. Hudson et al., *Sex and World Peace*.

322. Lerner, *Creation of Patriarchy*, 228–29.

323. Everdell, *First Moderns*, 6–12.

324. Zukov, *Dancing Wu Li Masters*, 63.

325. Three years after Einstein's special theory of relativity was formulated in 1905, the mathematician Hermann Minkowski, building on his former student's insight, declared, "Gentlemen! The views of space and time which I want to present to you arose from the domain of experimental physics, and therein lies their strength. Their tendency is radical. From now onwards space by itself and time by itself will recede completely to become mere shadows and only a type of union of the two will still stand independently on its own." Minkowski, *Space and Time*, 39. The "space-time continuum" consists of three dimensions of space plus a fourth dimension, time.

326. Sen, *Identity and Violence*, xii.

327. Bakan, *Duality of Human Existence*, 14–15.

328. Mishnah, *Sanhedrin*, 4:5.

Afterword

329. Shawn Eyer, email message to author, December 24, 2008.

330. Collio, *Cenni Biografici di*, 4.

331. Sotheby, Wilkinson, and Hodge, *Catalogue of the Extensive*.

332. Ps 118:22.

333. Lanci, *La sacra scrittura*, 27.

334. Lanci, *Paralipomeni*, xv.

335. Lanci, *Paralipomeni*, 101.

336. Lanci, *Paralipomeni*, 106.

337. Regarding verse 5, see Lanci, *Paralipomeni*, 107; regarding verse 19, see Lanci, *Paralipomeni*, 109.

338. Lanci, *Paralipomeni*, 121.

339. Lanci, *Paralipomeni*, 131.

340. Lanci, *Paralipomeni*, 240.

341. For his comments on the tetragrammaton, see Lanci, xiii, 101, 105–7, 114, 121, 128, 131, 183, 211, 215, 240, 254, 260.

342. Pius IX, *Qui Pluribus*.

343. Nott and Gliddon, *Types of Mankind*, 506 (Gliddon was the former U.S. Counsel to Cairo; his coauthor, Nott, was a medical doctor); Gliddon here identifies Lanci as "for 39 years 'Professor of Sacred Philology' at the Vatican" (Gliddon, *Otia Aegyptiaca*, 112); Burr, "Lanci's Letter, 177–83.

344. Lanci, *Lettre sur l'interprétation*, 1–4.

345. Lanci, *Lettre sur l'interprétation*, 17–20.

346. Lanci, *Lettre sur l'interprétation*, 192.

347. Tocqueville, *Recollections*, 98.

348. Burr, "Lanci's Letter," 177–83.

349. Burr wrote *Sagra*, but should have written *Sacra*.

350. Burr, "Lanci's Letter," 177–83.

351. For a list of his works, see http://www.masonicdictionary.com/mackey.html.

352. Mackey, *Lexicon of Freemasonry*, 156.

353. Mackey, *Symbolism of Freemasonry*, 185–86.

354. Mackey, *Symbolism of Freemasonry*, 186–89.

355. By Lanci's time, Kabbalistic works had been read by the non-Jewish intelligentsia for hundreds of years. Elia del Medigo had translated Hebrew texts into Latin for the Renaissance humanist Pico della Mirandola; his work attracted the attention of Sixtus IV (pope from 1471 to 1484) who, in turn, reportedly had some seventy Kabbalistic works translated into Latin. Postel was responsible for a Latin translation of the Zohar. Leibniz and Locke and others studied and appropriated Jewish Kabbalistic texts available in Latin translation. Lanci would have been able to read the works in the original Hebrew.

356. Wilkinson, *Tetragrammaton*, 335–37.

357. According to the Masonic writer Reid McInvale, "after Freemasonry became known to the world at large in the early eighteenth century the church took notice of it, and objected to it. Eight popes have issued pronouncements either explicitly condemning Freemasons or those activities and principles identified with Freemasonry." McInvale, *Roman Catholic*. The first pronouncement was Pope Clement XII's *In Eminenti* on April 28, 1738. The most recent pronouncement is "Declaration on Masonic" by Cardinal Joseph Ratzinger (later Pope Benedict XVI) on November 26, 1983.

ENDNOTES

358. His name is sometimes transliterated as Briullov or Briuloff. An image of the painting is sometimes posted online by dealers in art reproductions.
359. New York Historical Society, "Michelangelo Lanci."

Bibliography

Allen, James P. *The Ancient Egyptian Pyramid Texts*, Atlanta: Society of Biblical Literature, 2005.
Alter, Robert. *The Art of Biblical Narrative*. New York: Basic Books, 1981.
Ashtor, Eliyahu. "Spain." In *Encyclopedia Judaica*, edited by Cecil Roth and Geoffrey Wigoder, 15:220–46. Jerusalem: Keter, 1972.
Assaf, Simha, and Jehoshuah Brand. "Gaon." In *Encyclopedia Judaica*, edited by Cecil Roth and Geoffrey Wigoder, 7:315–24. Jerusalem: Keter, 1972.
Bakan, David. *The Duality of Human Existence: An Essay on Psychology and Religion*. Chicago: McNally, 1966.
Barthes, Roland. *S/Z*. NY: Hill and Wang, 1974.
Benisch, Abraham. *The Pentateuch and the Haftaroth, Newly Translated Under the Supervision of the Rev. the Chief Rabbi of the United Congregations of the British Empire, the Fourth Book of Moses*. 3rd ed. Rodelheim: Lehrberger, 1889.
Birnbaum, Philip, trans. *Daily Prayer Book*, Ha-Siddur Ha-Shalem. New York: Hebrew Publishing, 1995.
Blenkinsopp, Joseph. *The Pentateuch: An Introduction to the First Five Books of the Bible*. New York: Doubleday, 1992.
Brettler, Marc Tzvi. "Kabbalat Shabbat: A Liturgy from Psalms." In *My People's Prayer Book: Traditional Prayers, Modern Commentaries*, edited by Lawrence A. Hoffman, 21–26. Woodstock: Jewish Lights, 2005.
Broome, Edwin. "Ezekiel's Abnormal Personality." *Journal of Biblical Literature* 65 (1946) 277–84.
Brown, Francis, et al. *A Hebrew and English Lexicon of the Old Testament Based on the Lexicon of William Gesenius*. Oxford: Oxford University Press, 1952.
Browning, Frank. *The Fate of Gender: Nature, Nurture, and the Human Future*. New York: Bloomsbury, 2016.
Buber, Martin. "The Spirit of the Orient and Judaism." In *On Judaism*, edited by Nahum N. Glatzer, 56–78. New York: Schocken, 1967.
Burr, Charles Chauncey, ed. "Lanci's Letter to Prisse." *The Nineteenth Century: A Quarterly Miscellany* 2 (January 1848) 177–83.

BIBLIOGRAPHY

Carr, David M. "Changes in Pentateuchal Criticism." In *Hebrew Bible/Old Testament III: From Modernism to Post-Modernism; Part II: The Twentieth Century—From Modernism to Post-Modernism*, edited by Magne Saeboe, 433–66. Göttingen: Vandenhoeck and Ruprecht, 2014.

Cassuto, Umberto. *The Documentary Hypothesis and the Composition of the Pentateuch: Eight Lectures by Umberto Cassuto*. Jerusalem: Shalem, 2006.

Central Conference of American Rabbis. *The Union Prayerbook for Jewish Worship*. Vol. 1. New York: 1961.

Conkey, Margaret W. "A History of the Interpretation of European 'Paleolithic Art': Magic, Mythogram, and Metaphors for Modernity." In *The Handbook of Human Symbolic Evolution*, edited by Andrew Lock and Charles R. Peters, 288–349. Oxford: Oxford University Press, 1996.

Collio, Servino Servanzi. *Cenni Biografici di Michelangelo Lanci*. Macerata: Presso Alessandro Mancini, 1839.

Coulton, G. G. *Medieval Panorama: The English Scene from Conquest to Reformation*, New York: Cambridge University Press, 2010.

Cross, Frank Moore. *Canaanite Myth and Hebrew Epic*. Cambridge: Harvard University Press, 1973.

Daly, Mary. *Beyond God the Father: Toward a Philosophy of Women's Liberation*. Boston: Beacon, 1973.

Dan, Joseph, *The Early Kabbalah*. New York: Paulist, 1986.

Dan, Joseph, ed. *Jewish Mysticism*. Vol. 2, *The Middle Ages*. Northvale, NJ: Aronson, 1998.

Dever, William G. *Did God Have a Wife? Archeology and Folk Religion in Ancient Israel*. Grand Rapids: Eerdmans, 2008.

———. *Who Were the Early Israelites and Where Did They Come From?* Grand Rapids: Eerdmans, 2003.

De Vidas, Elijah ben Moses. *The Beginning of Wisdom: Unabridged Translation of the Gates of Love from Rabbi Elijah ben Moses de Vidas' Reishit Chokhmah*. Translated by Simcha H. Benyosef. Brooklyn: KTAV, 2001.

Diamond, Jared. *Guns, Germs, and Steel: The Fates of Human Societies*. New York: Norton, 1997.

Doherty, Cha. "The Trayf Jew." In *Balancing on the Mechitza: Transgender in the Jewish Community*, edited by Noach Dzmura, 12–22. Berkeley: North Atlantic, 2010.

Dorman, Peter F. "Akhenaten: King of Egypt." https://www.britannica.com/biography/Akhenaten.

Drob, Sanford L. "The Doctrine of *Coincidentia Oppositorum* in Jewish Mysticism." https://www.scribd.com/document/269399603/The-Doctrine-of-Coincidentia-Oppositorum-in-Jewish-Mysticism.

Durant, Will. *The Story of Civilization. Vol. 1, Our Oriental Heritage*. New York: Simon and Schuster, 1935.

Elbogen, Ismar. *Jewish Liturgy: A Comprehensive History*. Translated by Raymond P. Scheindlin. Philadelphia: Jewish Publication Society, 1993.

BIBLIOGRAPHY

"Enmerkar and the Lord of Aratta." http://etcsl.orinst.ox.ac.uk/section1/tr1823.htm.

Everdell, William R. *The First Moderns: Profiles in the Origins of Twentieth-Century Thought.* Chicago: University of Chicago Press, 1997.

Fishbane, Eitan P. "The Zohar: Masterpiece of Jewish Mysticism." In *Jewish Mysticism and Kabbalah: New Insights and Scholarship*, edited by Frederick E. Greenspahn, 49–67, New York: New York University Press, 2011.

Fishman, Seth. "El Mistater." https://www.jewishrenewalhasidus.org/el-mistater.

Friedman, H., and Maurice Simon, eds. and trans. *Midrash Rabbah.* London: Soncino, 1961.

Friedman, Richard Elliott. *Who Wrote the Bible?* New York: HarperCollins, 1997.

Frymer-Kenksy, Tikva. *In the Wake of the Goddesses: Women, Culture, and the Biblical Transformation of Pagan Myth.* New York: Free Press, 1992.

Gikatilla, Joseph ben Abraham. *Gates of Light: Sha'are Orah.* Translated by Avi Weinstein. New York: HarperCollins, 1994.

Ginzberg, Louis. *The Legend of the Jews.* Philadelphia: Jewish Publication Society of America, 1968.

Gliddon, George Robbins. *Otia Aegyptiaca: Discourses on Egyptian Archaeology and Hieroglyphical Discoveries.* London: Madden, 1849.

Gombrich, Ernst. "The Miracle at Chauvet." *The New York Review of Books*, November 14, 1996.

Gottlieb, Efraim. "Nahmanides." In *Encyclopedia Judaica*, edited by Cecil Roth and Geoffrey Wigoder, 12:774–82. Jerusalem: Keter, 1972.

Graves, Michael. "The Origins of *Ketiv-Qere* Readings." *TC: A Journal of Biblical Criticism* 8 (2003). http://www.jbtc.org/v08/Graves2003.html.

Green, Arthur. "Introduction." In *The Zohar: Pritzker Edition*, by Daniel C. Matt, 1:xxvii–lxxvii. Stanford: Stanford University Press, 2004.

Green, Arthur, and Barry Holtz, trans. *Your Word Is Fire: The Chassidic Masters on Contemplative Prayer.* Woodstock: Jewish Lights, 1993.

Green, Arthur, et al., eds. *Speaking Torah: Spiritual Teachings from Around the Maggid's Table.* Vol. 1. Woodstock: Jewish Lights, 2013.

Hadley, Judith M. *The Cult of Asherah in Ancient Israel and Judah: Evidence for a Hebrew Goddess.* Cambridge: Cambridge University Press, 2000.

Halevi, Judah. *The Kuzari: In Defense of The Despised Faith.* Translated and annotated by N. Daniel Korobkin. Northvale, NJ: Jason Aronson, 1998.

Harper, Robert Francis, ed. *Assyrian and Babylonian Literature: Selected Translations.* New York: D. Appleton, 1901.

Hellner-Eshed, Melila. *A River Flows From Eden: The Language of Mystical Experience in the Zohar.* Stanford: Stanford University Press, 2009.

Herr, Moshe David. "Exodus Rabbah." In *Encyclopedia Judaica*, edited by Cecil Roth and Geoffrey Wigoder, 6:1067–69. Jerusalem: Keter, 1972.

Hoffman, Joel M. *In the Beginning: A Short History of the Hebrew Language.* New York: New York University Press, 2004.

Hopkins, Jasper. *Nicholas of Cusa on Learned Ignorance: A Translation and an Appraisal of* De Docta Ignorantia. 2nd ed. Minneapolis: Arthur Manning, 1985. http://jasper-hopkins.info/DI-Intro12-2000.pdf.

Horowitz, Maryanne Cline. "The Image of God in Man—Is Woman Included?" *Harvard Theological Review* 72.3–4 (1979) 175–206.

Hudson, Valerie M., et al. *Sex and World Peace*. New York: Columbia University Press, 2012.

Idel, Moshe. "Defining Kabbalah: The Kabbalah of the Divine Names." In *Mystics of the Book: Themes, Topics, and Typologies*, edited by Robert A. Herrera, 97–117. New York: Lang, 1993.

———. *Kabbalah and Eros*. New Haven: Yale University Press, 2005.

———. *Kabbalah: New Perspectives*. New Haven: Yale University Press, 1988.

Israel Museum. "Hebrew Letter." https://www.imj.org.il/en/collections/369574.

Israel Museum. "Hebrew Letter (Ostracon)." https://www.imj.org.il/en/collections/394413.

Israel Museum. "'Priestly Benediction' on Amulets." https://www.imj.org.il/en/collections/198069.

Josephus, Flavius. "The Wars of the Jews: Or History of the Destruction of Jerusalem." In *The Works of Flavius Josephus*, translated by William Whiston, 480–678. London: Routledge, n.d. https://archive.org/details/worksofflaviusjo1873jose/page/n3.

Joyce, James. *Ulysses*. New York: Vintage, 1961.

Kaplan, Aryeh. *Meditation and Kabbalah*. San Francisco: Weiser Books, 1982.

Kaplan, Aryeh, trans. and ed. *The Bahir: A Translation and Commentary*. Northvale, NJ: Aronson, 1995.

———. *Sefer Yetzirah: The Book of Creation*. Northvale, NJ: Aronson, 1995.

Killermann, Sam. *A Guide to Gender: The Social Justice Advocate's Handbook*. 2nd ed. Austin: Impetus, 2013.

King, Leonard William. *The Seven Tablets of Creation*. Charleston, SC: BiblioLife, 2008.

Kuenen, Abraham. *The Religion of Israel to the Fall of the Jewish State*. Vol. 1. Translated by Alfred Heath May. London: Williams and Norgate, 1874.

Kugel, James L. *The Bible As It Was*. Cambridge: Harvard University Press, 1997.

Lanci, Michelangelo. *La sacra scrittura illustrata con monumenti fenico-assirj ed egiziani*. Rome: Dalla Societa Tipografica, 1827.

———. *Lettre sur l'interprétation des Hiéroglyphes Égyptiens, adressée* à M. Prisse d'Avennes. Paris: Librairie Scientifique, Francaise et Orientale, 1847.

———. *Paralipomeni alla Illustrazione della Sagra Scrittura Monumenti Fenico-Assirii ed Egiziana*. Paris: Dondey-Dupre, 1845.

Lante, L. *Michelangelo Lanci, Object Number X.76*. Portrait bust, 18.4 × 11.1 × 8.6 cm. New York Historical Society. https://www.nyhistory.org/exhibit/michelangelo-lanci.

Leeser, Isaac. *The Twenty-Four Books of the Holy Scriptures: Carefully Translated According to the Masoretic Text, After the Best Jewish Authorities*. Cincinnati: American Hebrew, 1853.

BIBLIOGRAPHY

Leeser, Isaac, ed. *The Law of God.* Vol. 4, *The Book of Numbers.* Philadelphia: Sherman, 1845.

Leiman, Shnayer Z., ed. *The Canon and Masorah of the Hebrew Bible: An Introductory Reader.* New York: KTAV, 1974.

Lerner, Gerda. *The Creation of Patriarchy.* New York: Oxford University Press, 1986.

Leroi-Gourhan, André. *The Dawn of European Art: An Introduction to Palaeolithic Cave Painting.* Cambridge: Cambridge University Press, 1982.

Leuenberger, Martin. "YHWH's Provenance from the South: A New Evaluation of the Arguments Pro and Contra." In *The Origins of Yahwism,* edited by Jurgen van Oorschot and Markus Witte, 157–79. Berlin: De Gruyter, 2017.

Lévi-Strauss, Claude. *The Raw and the Cooked: Introduction to a Science of Mythology.* Vol. 1. New York: Harper and Row, 1969.

Lieber, David L., ed. *Etz Hayim: Torah and Commentary.* New York: Jewish Publication Society, 2004.

Liebus, Esther (Zweig). "Isaac the Blind." In *Encyclopedia Judaica,* edited by Cecil Roth and Geoffrey Wigoder, 9:35–36. Jerusalem: Keter, 1972.

Louvre. "The Mesha Stele." https://www.louvre.fr/en/oeuvre-notices/mesha-stele.

Mackey, Albert G. *A Lexicon of Freemasonry: Containing a Definition of All Its Communicable Terms, Notices of its History, Traditions, and Antiquities, and an Account of All of the Rites and Mysteries of the Ancient World.* London and Glasgow: Richard Griffin and Company. 1860.

———. *Symbolism of Freemasonry: Illustrating and Explaining Its Science, Philosophy, Legends, Myths, and Symbols.* New York: Clark and Maynard, 1869.

Magid, Shaul. "The Rebbe of the Warsaw Ghetto." *Tablet Magazine,* April 7, 2017. http://www.tabletmag.com/jewish-arts-and-culture/228300/the-rebbe-of-the-warsaw-ghetto.

Maimonides, Moses. *The Guide for the Perplexed.* Translated by M. Friedlander. 2nd ed. London: Routledge and Kegan Paul, 1951.

Mantel, Hugo. "Sanhedrin." In *Encyclopedia Judaica,* edited by Cecil Roth and Geoffrey Wigoder, 14:836–39. Jerusalem: Keter, 1972.

Matt, Daniel C. *The Essential Kabbalah.* San Francisco: HarperCollins, 1996.

———. *The Zohar: Pritzker Edition.* vols. 1-3, Stanford: Stanford University Press, 2004–6.

McInvale, Reid. "Roman Catholic Church Law Regarding Freemasonry." http://www.bessel.org/cathtlor.htm.

Meshel, Ze'ev. "Did Yahweh Have a Consort? The New Religious Inscriptions from the Sinai." *Biblical Archeology Review* 5 (1979) 24–34.

Milgrom, Jacob. *The JPS Torah Commentary: Numbers.* Philadelphia: Jewish Publication Society, 1990.

Minkowski, Hermann. *Space and Time: Minkwoski's Papers on Relativity.* Translated by Fritz Lewertoff and Vesselin Petkov, edited by Vesselin Petkov. Montreal: Minkowski Institute, 2016.

Mommsen, Theodore E. "Petrarch's Conception of the 'Dark Ages.'" *Speculum* 17.2 (April 1942) 226–42.
Moore, George F. "Notes on the Name [*Yod Heh Vov Heh*]." *American Journal of Theology* 12 (January 1908) 34–52.
Morgenstern, Julian. "The Mythological Background of Psalm 82." *Hebrew Union College Annual* 14 (1939) 29–126.
Munk, Eliyahu, trans. *Torah Commentary by Rabbi Bachya ben Asher*. Vol. 1. Jerusalem: Urim, 2003.
Murray, M. A. "The Name of Ra." In *Ancient Egyptian Legends*, edited by L. Cranmer-Byng, 80–86. London: Murray, 1920.
Najman, Hindy. "Nehemiah." In *The Jewish Study Bible*, edited by Adele Berlin and Marc Zvi Brettler, 1688–711. Oxford: Oxford University Press, 2004.
Nachod, Hans. "On His Own Ignorance and That of Many Others." In *The Renaissance Philosophy of Man*, edited by Ernst Cassirer, P.O. Kristeller, and J. H. Randall, Jr., 47–133. Chicago: Chicago University Press, 1948.
Nott, Josiah Clark, and George Robins Gliddon. *Types of Mankind: Ethnological Researches Based Upon the Ancient Monuments, Paintings, Sculptures, and Crania of Races, and Upon Their Natural, Geographical, Philological, and Biblical History*. Philadelphia: Lippincott, Grambo, 1854.
Oorschot, Jurgen van, and Markus Witte, eds. *The Origins of Yahwism*. Berlin: De Gruyter, 2017.
Origen. *Contra Celsum*. In *The Ante-Nicene Fathers: The Writings of the Fathers Down to A.D. 325*, translated by Frederick Crombie and edited by Alexander Roberts et al., 4:395–669. Buffalo: Christian Literature, 1885.
Parke-Taylor, G. H. *Yahweh: The Divine Name in the Bible*. Waterloo, ON: Wilfrid Laurier University Press, 1975.
Pew Research Center. "'Nones' on the Rise." http://www.pewforum.org/2012/10/09/nones-on-the-rise/.
———. "Religion in Everyday Life." http://www.pewforum.org/2016/04/12/religion-in-everyday-life/.
Pietersma, Albert, and Benjamin G. Wright, eds. *A New English Translation of the Septuagint*. Oxford: Oxford University Press, 2007.
Pius IX, Pope. *Qui Pluribus: On Faith and Religion*. http://www.papalencyclicals.net/Pius09/p9quiplu.htm.
Plaut, Gunther, ed. *The Haftarah Commentary*. Translated by Chaim Stern. New York: UAHC, 1996.
Plaut, W. Gunther, and David E. S. Stein, eds. *The Torah: A Modern Commentary, Revised Edition*. New York: Central Conference of American Rabbis, 2006.
Pogrebin, Letty Cottin. *Deborah, Golda, and Me: Being Female and Jewish in America*. New York: Crown, 1991.
Polen, Nehemia. *The Holy Fire: The Teachings of Rabbi Kalonymus Kalman Shapira, the Rebbe of the Warsaw Ghetto*. Northvale, NJ: Aronson, 1999.
Porten, Bezalel. *The Elephantine Papyri in English: Three Millennia of Cross-Cultural Continuity and Change*. New York: Brill, 1996.

BIBLIOGRAPHY

Rainey, Anson F. "Israel in Merenptah's Inscription and Reliefs." *Israel Exploration Journal* 51.2 (2001) 57–75.

Rashi. *Chumash with Rashi's Commentary.* Vol. 2, *Shemoth.* Edited by A. M. Silbermann. Jerusalem: Feldheim, 1934.

Ratzinger, Joseph Card. "Declaration on Masonic Associations." Palace of the Holy Office, Rome: Congregation for the Doctrine of the Faith, November 26, 1983. http://www.vatican.va/roman_curia/congregations/cfaith/documents/rc_con_cfaith_doc_19831126_declaration-masonic_en.html.

Redford, Donald B. *Egypt, Canaan, and Israel in Ancient Times.* Princeton: Princeton University Press, 1992.

Rosman, Moshe. *Founder of Hasidism: A Quest for the Historical Ba'al Shem Tov.* 2nd ed. Oxford: Littman Library of Jewish Civilization, 2013.

Russell, Michael. *A Connection of Sacred and Profane History: From the Death of Joshua to the Decline of the Kingdoms of Israel and Judah.* Vol. 1. London: Tegg, 1860.

Safrai, S. "The Era of the Mishnah and Talmud (70–640)." In *A History of the Jewish People,* edited by H. H. Ben-Sasson, 307–82. Cambridge: Harvard University Press, 1976.

Sameth, Mark. "God's Hidden Name Revealed." *Reform Judaism Magazine,* Spring 2009.

———. "Is God Transgender?" *New York Times,* August 12, 2016.

———. "This Dor Swings Both Ways: Judah's Bisexuality." *CCAR Journal: A Reform Jewish Quarterly* 66.1 (Winter 2019) 84–91.

———. "Who Is He? He Is She: The Secret Four-Letter Name of God." *CCAR Journal: A Reform Jewish Quarterly* 55.3 (Summer 2008) 22–28.

Sammons, Benjamin. "History and *Hyponoia*: Herodutus and Early Literary Criticism." *Histos* 6 (2012) 52–66.

Sarna, Nahum M. "Excursus 25: The Name 'Israel.'" In *The JPS Torah Commentary.* Vol. 1, *Genesis.* Philadelphia: Jewish Publication Society, 1989.

Schama, Simon. *The Story of the Jews: Finding the Words, 1000 BC–1492 AD.* New York: HarperCollins, 2013.

Scholem, Gershom. "Ba'al Shem." In *Encyclopedia Judaica,* edited by Cecil Roth and Geoffrey Wigoder, 4:5–7. Jerusalem: Keter, 1972.

———. "Jacob ben Jacob Ha-Kohen." In *Encyclopedia Judaica,* edited by Cecil Roth and Geoffrey Wigoder, 9:1219–20. Jerusalem: Keter, 1972.

———."Kabbalah." In *Encyclopedia Judaica,* edited by Cecil Roth and Geoffrey Wigoder, 10:489–653. Jerusalem: Keter, 1972.

———. "The Name of God and the Linguistic Theory of the Kabbala (Part 2)." *Diogenes* 20.80 (December 1972) 164–94.

———. *Kabbalah.* New York: Quadrangle, 1974.

———. *Major Trends in Jewish Mysticism.* New York: Schocken, 1995.

———. *On the Kabbalah and Its Symbolism.* New York: Schocken, 1969.

———. *Origins of the Kabbalah.* Edited by R. J. Werblowsky and translated by Allan Arkush. Philadelphia: Jewish Publication Society, 1987.

BIBLIOGRAPHY

———. *Sabbatai Sevi: The Mystical Messiah 1626–1676*. Princeton: Princeton University Press, 1973.
Segran, Elizabeth. "The Rise of the Islamic Feminists." *The Nation*, December 4, 2013.
Seltzer, Robert M. *Jewish People, Jewish Thought: The Jewish Experience in History*. New York: Macmillan, 1980.
Sen, Amartya. *Identity and Violence: The Illusion of Destiny*. New York: Norton, 2006.
Shaked, Shaul, et al. *Aramaic Bowl Spells: Jewish Babylonian Aramaic Bowls*. Vol. 1, *Magical and Religious Literature of Late Antiquity*. Leiden: Brill, 2013.
Shannon-Missal, Larry. "Americans' Belief in God, Miracles, and Heaven Declines." https://theharrispoll.com/new-york-n-y-december-16-2013-a-new-harris-poll-finds-that-while-a-strong-majority-74-of-u-s-adults-do-believe-in-god-this-belief-is-in-decline-when-compared-to-previous-years-as-just-over/.
Shapira, Kalonymos Kalman. *Sacred Fire: Torah from the Years of Fury, 1939–1942*. Translated by J. Hershy Worch and edited by Deborah Miller. Lanham: Rowman and Littlefield, 2002.
Sharabi, Shalom. *Siddur Kavanot HaRashash*. Jerusalem: Yeshivat HaChaim Ve'Hashalom, 2002.
Silvers, Laury and Ahmed Elewa. "'I Am One of the People': A Survey and Analysis of Legal Arguments on Woman-Led Prayer in Islam." *Journal of Law and Religion* 26.1 (January 4, 2011) 141–71.
Smith, W. Robertson. *The Old Testament in the Jewish Church: A Course of Lectures on Biblical Criticism*. New York: Appleton, 1882.
Sotheby, et al. *Catalogue of the Extensive and Valuable Library of Manuscripts and Printed Books of His Excellency Monsieur John Gennadius [. . .]*. London: Dryden, 1895.
Stein, David E. S. "The Noun איש ('îš) in Biblical Hebrew: A Term of Affiliation." *Journal of Hebrew Scriptures* 8.1 (2008). doi:10.5508/jhs.2008.v8.a1.
Tadmor, H. "The Period of the First Temple, the Babylonian Exile, and the Restoration." In *A History of the Jewish People*, edited by H. H. Ben-Sasson, 91–182. Cambridge: Harvard University Press, 1976.
Thomas, David Hurst, and Robert L. Kelly. *Archaeology*. Belmont, CA: Thomson Wadsworth, 2006.
Tocqueville, Alexis de. *Recollections: The French Revolution of 1848*. Garden City, NY: Doubleday, 1970.
Toorn, Karel van der. *Scribal Culture and the Making of the Hebrew Bible*. Cambridge: Harvard University Press, 2007.
Uffenheimer, Rivka Schatz. *Hasidism as Mysticism: Quietistic Elements in Eighteenth Century Hasidic Thought*. Translated by Jonathan Chipman. Princeton: Princeton University Press; 1993.
Wellhausen, Julius. *Israelitische und Jüdischer Geschichte*. Berlin: Reimer, 1894.
Whybray, R. N. *The Making of the Pentateuch: A Methodological Study*. New York: Sheffield Academic Press, 1987.

BIBLIOGRAPHY

Wilkinson, Robert J. *Tetragrammaton: Western Christians and the Hebrew Name of God.* Boston: Brill, 2015.

Wolfson, Elliot R. *Circle in the Square: Studies in the Use of Gender in Kabbalistic Symbolism.* Albany: State University of New York Press, 1995.

———. "Constructions of the Shekhinah in the Messianic Theosophy of Abraham Cardoso with an Annotated Edition of *Derush ha-Shekhinah.*" *Kabbalah: A Journal for the Study of Jewish Mystical Texts* 3 (1998) 11–143.

———. *Language, Eros, Being: Kabbalistic Hermeneutics and Poetic Imagination.* New York: Fordham University Press, 2004.

Wright, Daniel P. *The Disposal of Impurity: Elimination Rites in the Bible and in Hittite and Mesopotamian Literature.* SBLDS 101. Atlanta: Scholars, 1987.

Wright, Robert. *The Evolution of God.* New York: Little, Brown, 2009.

Xenophon. *Memorabilia, Oeconomicus, Symposium, Apology.* Translated by E. C. Marchant and O. J. Todd. Cambridge: Harvard University Press, 1923.

Zukov, Gary. *The Dancing Wu Li Masters: An Overview of the New Physics.* New York: Bantam, 1980.

Index

Aaron, 35, 128n88
Aaron of Baghdad (Abu Aaron), 50–51, 90
Abba (name for God), 303
Abba (rabbi), 73, 137n242
Abayye, 120n27, 141n294
Abishai, 44–45
Abram, 34, 124n71, 129n103
Abraham, ix, 25, 34–35, 121n38, 129n103
Abraham ben David of Posquieres (Rabad), 63
Abravanel, Isaac, 128n77
Abu Aaron. *See* Aaron of Baghdad
Abulafia, Abraham ben Samuel: Or ha-Sekhel (Light of the Intellect), 68–70, 136n218
Acher, 67
adam: and Eve, 40, 60, 104; in image of God, 94, 106; intersex, 39–40, 56, 125n71, 133n164; sin of, 75; as "them," 32, 125n71; Torah in language of, 98
Adonai, 2–3, 117n5, 121n38. *See also* substitute names for God
Ahilai, 56
Akhenaten, Pharaoh, 12
alef: Abulafia on missing letter, 68; in *bo*, 138n260; in Genesis 1:1, 138n259; in *hi*, 123n71, 124n71; in *hu*, 140nn287–288; Jacob ben Sheshet on disappearing letter, 136n216; male letter, 137n242; meditation on, 65, 84; missing from *anachnu*, 136n217; Rashi on missing letter, 69; in *yisrael*, 129n103
Akiva, 67, 131n140
Akkadian: civilization, 10; hybrids, 14; language, 119n22
allegory: Adam and Eve as, 98, 106; Bible stories as, 27; myths as, 98; need for, 105
Alter, Robert, 37, 38
Alkabetz, Shlomo ha-Levi: *Lecha Dodi*, 80, 89
Almohad, 54
alz ist Gott, 90–91
Amarah-West, 120n29
Amenhotep III, Pharaoh, 18
Amidah, 46, 76
Amittai Ba'al Shem, 51
Amram, 34
apocatastasis, 79
Arabic, 49, 107; relative pronouns in, 59
Arabian Peninsula, 50
Arad: pottery of, 24
Ashera (goddess), 9, 118n14
asherah (cultic object), 118n14
Ashkenazi(m), 50

157

INDEX

Ashur, 31
Asher ben David, 65
Assyrian, 28; army, 31; block script, 30–32; civilization, 10; king, 31
Atbash, 5
Aten, 12
av bet din, 46, 131n127
Av Kol ha-Sodot. *See* Aaron of Baghdad
Avinu Malkenu, 9
avodah b'gashmiut, 86
Azriel of Gerona, 65

Ba'alei Masorah (Masoretes), 3, 127n77
Ba'alei Shem (Masters of THE NAME): names of, 85, 140n289
Amittai Ba'al Shem, 51
Ba'al Shem Tov (Israel ben Eliezer), 84–87, 95
Babylonian Talmud, 42, 46, 48–49, 82; academy, 52
Bachya ben Asher, 77, 135n200
Baghdad, 14, 43, 50–51, 60, 90
Bahir. *See* Book of Bright Light
Bar Kokhba Revolt, 44
Ben Azzai, 67
Ben Sira, 32–33, 39, 127n75
Ben Zoma, 67
Benedict XVI (pope), 144n357
Benisch, Abraham, 126n71
Benjamin, 35
bet (letter): in *bo*,138n260; as dual-gender, 56; as female, 137n242; in opening words of Torah, 138n259
Bet El, 83
Beta Yisrael, 50
Black Plague, 78
Boaz, greeting with THE NAME, 25
Book of Bright Light (Sefer ha-Bahir), 53–57, 61, 63–64, 95
Book of the Covenant (Sefer ha-Brit), 29–30

Book of Formation (Sefer Yetzirah), 46, 51, 55, 131n133, 131n140
Book of Speculation (Sefer ha-Iyyun), 64
Book of Splendor. *See Zohar* (mystical work)
Book of THE NAME (Sefer HaShem), 61, 134n191
Book of the Teaching (Sefer ha-Torah), 29
Book of Wisdom (Sefer ha-Chokhmah), 61
Babylonia: Aaron of Baghdad, 50; Agushaya Hymn of, 11; army of, 29, 31; demons in, 49; exile in, 29–31; Enuma Elish creation myth of, 13; Ezekiel in, 46; exilarch of, 46; Hai Gaon of, 52; Ishtar of, 11; Jeremiah and, 5; Jewish center of, 43, 45–46, 50; Judah as vassal state of, 29; magic in, 45; Marduk of, 10; Nehardea academy of, 46; pronunciation of THE NAME following return from, 1; Pumbedita academy of, 52; Rava of, 48; Saadiah Gaon of, 51; shamanic Jews of, 48; Sura academy of, 46; Talmud of, 42, 47, 82; Torah redacted in and brought from, x, 30, 94
binity, 21, 60
blood libel, 54
bride, God as, 54, 56, 75, 80, 133n164
Bryullov, Karl, 115
Buber, Martin, 88, 141n291, 141n299
Burr, Charles Chauncey, 112–13

Caesarea, 43
Cairo, 57, 113

INDEX

calendar, 72–73
Cardoso, Abraham Miguel, 82
Cassuto, Umberto, 37, 130n106
CCAR Journal, 8
Central Conference of American Rabbis, 8
Champollion, Jean-François, 111
Chanina, 45, 46, 80, 94
Chanina ben Teradyon, 130n125
Charlemagne, 51
Chinese Jews (Tiao Jin Jiao), 50
Chiyya, 47, 76, 123n62
Christianity: and blood libel against Jews, 54, 78; Christian era, 21; Crusades, 54, 61; Fourth Lateran Council, 72; martial god in, 31; Masons and, 110; Origen and, 48; *Reconquista*, 72; Spain pre-, 79; Jewish god and, 109; and Jewish shamans, 49; and worship of male god, 55
Clement XII (pope), 144n357. See also *In Eminenti Catholic*
Cochin (Indian Jews), 50
coincidentia oppositorum, 65
Cologne (France), 54
commandment. See mitzvah
Concealments of the Torah. See *Sitrei Torah*
Concerning Secrets of the Universal Truth (*De arcanis catholicae veritatis*) (Galatinus), 3–4
Córdoba (Spain): Maimonides born in, 57; Berber sacking of, 72
Crenshaw, Kimberlé Williams, 104
Chronicles (*Paralipomeni alla Illustrazione della Sagra Scrittura Monumenti Fenico-Assirii ed Egiziana*) (Lanci), 109
Cross, Frank Moore, 19
Crusades, 54, 61
cuneiform, 22

Dagger of Faith against the Moors and the Jews (*Pugio fidei adversus Mauros et Judaeos*) (Raymund Martin), 4
Daly, Mary, 99
Damasus I (pope), 2
Dark Ages, 54, 94
David, King, 7, 44–46; dynasty of, 28; Messiah from line of, 46; uttering THE NAME (miracle tale), 44–45
De arcanis catholicae veritatis (Galatinus), 3–4
Decretum, 133n160
demons, 45, 48–49, 54, 76, 91–2, 132n150
Deuteronomy, x, 29–30, 32, 35, 36, 66, 76–77
devekut, 87
Diamond, Jared, 20
Dinah, 34, 125n71
documentary hypothesis, 36; Alter and, 37; Astruc and, 36; Cassuto and, 37, 130n106; Graf and, 36; Wellhausen and, 36; Whybray and, 37
Dominus, 2,3. Also see substitute names for God
Dhul-Kifl, 47–48
Durant, Will, 10, 118n15

Eastern (Mizrachi) Jews, 50
Egypt, x, 2; dual-gender gods of, 10–13, 119n21; hieroglyphics of, 110–12; Maimonides in, 57. See also pharaohs
Egypt, Canaan, and Israel (Redford), 18
Ehyeh, 18, 84
Ehyeh Asher Ehyeh, 19, 59
Einstein, Albert, 104, 143n329
El Mistater, 142n306
Eleazar, son of Simon bar Yochai, 73, 76
Eleazar ben Judah of Worms, 61–62

159

INDEX

Elephantine Island, 19, 120n34
Eliezer of Damascus, 35
Elimelekh, son of Kalonymus
 Shapira, 92
Elohim, 36–37, 69, 108, 117n5,
 118n13
emanations. See sefirot
Enmerkar, 14, 119n23
Enuma Elish, 13, 118n20
enveloping light and penetrating
 light (ohr makif and ohr
 p'nini), 89
Esh Kodesh. See Holy Fire (Shapira)
Ethiopia, Jews of (Beta Yisrael), 50
Eve, 32–33, 40, 60, 104, 121n38,
 123n71
Everdell, William: First Moderns,
 103
"everything is God," 90–91
evil, 48–49, 54, 79, 91–92, 138n261,
 139n275
exilarch, office of, 46
Exodus, x, 5, 30, 34
Explanation of the Four-Lettered
 Name (Perush Shem shel
 Arba Otiyyot), 64
Eyer, Shawn, 143n329
Ezekiel, 46–48, 132n142; Dhul-Kifl
 as, 47–48. See also Workings
 of the Chariot
Ezra ha-Kohain, 30–31, 41, 94–95,
 123n64

"Father of All the Secrets." See
 Aaron of Baghdad
Ferdinand, King, 78
First Temple, 1, 46; period, 28–29
Five Books of Moses. See Pentateuch
folk etymologies, 19, 121n38
four-letter name of God. See
 tetragrammaton
France, x, 14, 53–54, 113
Freemasons. See Masons

gaon, title 46, 131n135. See also Hai
 Gaon; Saadiah Gaon; Vilna
 Gaon
Galatinus (Pietro Galitano):
 Concerning Secrets of the
 Universal Truth (De arcanis
 catholicae veritatis), 3–4
Galilee, 43–44
Galilean Sanhedrin, 44–45
Gamliel I, 44
gartel, 88
Gates of Light (Sha'are Orah)
 (Gikatilla), 69–71
gematria, 139n279
gender: equality, 102; expression,
 100; fluidity in the Bible 32;
 identity, 100; and peace, 102;
 revolution, 106; spectrum,
 100; in the Talmud, 100
Genesis, x, 25, 30, 39, 40, 47, 63, 71
German Pietists, 60, 94, 103,
 141n290
Germany, x, 5, 15, 51, 54, 60
Gerona (Spain), 64, 66; Azriel of,
 65; Jacob ben Sheshet of, 66;
 Nachmanides of, 67
Gesenius, Heinrich Friedrich
 Wilhelm: Hebrew and
 Aramaic Manual on the
 Old Testament (Hebräisches
 und Chaldäisches
 Handwörterbuch über das
 Alte Testament), 4
Gikatilla, Joseph ben Abraham:
 Gates of Light (Sha'are
 Orah), 69–71
Git'l, daughter-in-law of Kalonymus
 Shapira, 92
Gliddon, G. R., 113–14
Granada (Spain), 54, 72
Greek: 2, 107; allegory, 27; Astarte,
 11; Dominus (Lord), 2, 3;
 Empire, 41; encryption
 tool, scytale, 6; Homer,

INDEX

98; Kalonymus (name), 51; Minotaur, 15; nurse (*tithenos*), 120, 126; undermeanings (*hyponoiai*), 98; sacred marriage (*hieros gamos*), 89; symbol of phallus and *cteis*, 114; THE NAME not translated into, 49. *See also* Septuagint; Heraclitus

Greek Jews (Romaniote), 50

Guide for the Perplexed (Maimonides), 57–60

Ha Kadosh Boruch Hu, 80, 82

Haggadah, 85, 140n288

Hagar, 126n71

Hai Gaon, 52, 134n191

Halevi, Yehudah (Judah). *See* Judah Halevi

Hamnuna Sava, 76

Handel, G. F., 126n71

Harry Potter (novel), 27

Hayon, Gedaliah, 83

heh (letter): added to names Abram and Sarai, 55n122; added to YHW, 24–26; disagreement over, 124n71; in Eve's name, 123n71; of expanded name, 84; in hi, 8, 140n288; in hu, 8, 140n287; mater lectionis, 23; missing from na'ar, 124–125n71; of tetragrammaton, 8, 55, 77; in ohalo, 124n71; in yedidiah, 118n11

HaShem, ix, 2, 8. *See also* Sefer HaShem (book); *yichud HaShem* (unification); tetragrammaton

Hasidei Ashkenaz. *See* German Pietists

Hasidism, 86, 141n291; monist world-view of, 90–92; practices of, 87–88; rationale for not pronouncing THE NAME, 21. *See also* Ba'al Shem Tov

Hatshepsut, Pharaoh, 17

Hebrew and Aramaic Manual on the Old Testament (*Hebräisches und Chaldäisches Handwörterbuch über das Alte Testament*) (Gesenius), 4

Hebrew Bible (TaNaKh): allegories in, 27; composition of, 27, 30, 39, 98; dual-gender in, 8, 32, 41; first five books of, x, 28; heh (letter) in, 26; folk etymologies of, 19, 121n38; Kaufmann on, 19; Lanci and, 109; as literary work, 27; names for God in, 31, 57, 64; old and new forms of words in, 124n71; secrets in, 6–7, 48; typology in, 26; translation of, ix; and wordplay, 126n71; Zohar and, 74

Hebrew Union College–Jewish Institute of Religion, 4

Hegel, G. W. F., 119n26

Heraclitus of Ephesus 41, 132n142

hieroglyphics, 20, 22, 111

hieros gamos, 56, 89

high priest: 43; Hilkiah, 28; Pinchas ben Shmuel, 44; Rabbi Tarfon and, 44; Shimon ha-Tzaddik (Simon the Just), 1–2, 41

Hilkiah (high priest), 28

Hillel the Babylonian, 123n62

Hira, Judah and, 74

Hoffman, Joel: *In the Beginning*, 23, 26

Holocaust, x, 91–93

Holy Fire, The (Polen), 92

Holy Fire (Shapira), 91

INDEX

Holy of Holies: mystical meaning of, 56
Homer, 98, 142n312
Horowitz, Maryanne Cline: "The Image of God in Man," 40
Hu-Hi, ix, 8, 22, 23–24, 66, 68. *See also* names of God
Hudson, Valerie: *Sex and World Peace*, 102
Huldah, 29
husband, God as, 75
hybrids, 14–15. See also therianthropy; theriocephaly
hyponoiai, 98

ibn Ezra, Abraham, 23, 38, 121n47, 130n110,
Ibrahim ibn Adham, 52
incantation bowls, 48
Idel, Moshe, 134n191, 136n219, 138n272
ineffable name, 3, 114–15. *See also* tetragrammaton
In Eminenti Catholic, 144n357
Indian Jews (Cochin, Malabari), 50
integral philosophy, 104
intersectional theory, 104
Inyani bar Susai, 45
Isaac, 26, 34–35, 104n103
Isaac ben Jacob ha-Kohen, 68
Isaac Luria, 80–81, 83–87, 95
Isaac the Blind, 63–64, 66–68, 79
Isabella, Queen, 78
Isaiah: Book of, 17, 25, 32, 48, 69; THE NAME and miracle tale of, 48
ish, 74, 137n241
Ish Milchamah, 31, 123n68
Ishtar, 11
Islam: Almohad 54, 57, 72; Almoravids, 72: Berber, 72; Sufi, 52; Umayyad, 72
Israel: x, 1, 10, 17, 50; eighth century BCE, 19; meaning of name, 129n103; ninth century CE, 50; northern Kingdom of, 28; priests of, ix, 26; Ten Lost Tribes of, 28; united kingdom of, 28
Israel (Jacob): change of name, 34
Israel ben Eliezer. *See* Ba'al Shem Tov
Israel Museum, 24
Italkim (Italian Jews), 50
Italian Jews (Italkim), 50
Italy. *See* Italian Jews; Rome
Iudea, 43

Jacob, 26; and Esau, 76; and Laban, 35; and Rachel, 35
Jacob ben Jacob ha-Kohen, 65, 67–68, 81–82
Jacob ben Sheshet of Gerona, 66
Jehoiachin, King, 46
Jehovah, ix, 2–4, 114. *See also* names of God
Jeremiah, 5, 6, 25, 29, 64
Jeremiah b. Leazar, 40
Jerome, 2
Jerusalem Talmud, 47
Jethro, 34
Jezebel, Queen, 118n114
Jewish Publication Society, 33
Job, 54
Joel, 25
Jonah, 32
Joseph, 26; and the multi-colored coat, 74
Josiah, King, 28
Joyce, James: *Ulysses*, 38
Judah, Hira and, 74
Judah, southern kingdom of, 28–29, 31, 41
Judah the Pious of Regensburg (Yehudah he-Hasid aka Judah ben Samuel), 60–62, 64, 66, 94
Judah ha-Nasi, 44

INDEX

Judah Halevi, 23, 70–71, 86, 121n47; *Kuzari*, 52–53
Judah Maccabee, 50
Judaism: Abrahamic faith of, ix; binity and, 21; dissemination of esoteric knowledge in, 51; interpretative tradition of, ix; adherents to, xi; mainstream, 88; Wellhausen's aversion to, 130n111; Zohar, most holy book of, 133n162

Kabbalah: Abulafia's dissemination of, 68; beginning of, 53; Book of Bright Light, 53–57; Book of Speculation, 64; as response to history, 138n272; messianism and, 72; Maimonides's opposition to, 57–58; misinterpretation of, 68; Nachmanides's support of, 67; pre-Kabbalah mystics, 62. *See also* Lurianic Kabbalah; Zohar (mystical work)
Kaddish Yatom, 54
Kaufmann, Yehezkel, 18–19
kavvanah, 65, 80–81, 84–85, 139n279. *See also yichudim*
Ketina, Rav, 73
Khafre, Pharaoh, 14
King James Bible, 4, 69, 120n27, 126n71
Kings, Book of, 28–29, 123n58
kings of Judah: Asa, 118n14; Jehoiachin, 46; Josiah, 28–29; Manasseh, 118n14
kings of (the united kingdom of) Israel: David, 7, 44, 46; Solomon, 12, 28
kohanim. *See* priests
Kalonymus family. *See* Eleazar ben Judah of Worms; Judah the Pious of Regensburg; Kalonymus Kalman Shapira; Moses ben Kalonymus of Lucca
Kiddush ha-Chodesh, 136n233
"Kings Shall Be Thy Nursing Fathers," 126n71
Kuenen, Abraham, 19
Kugel, James, 32
Kurios (Kýrios), 2–3. *See also* substitute names (for God)
Kushner, Lawrence, xi, 4–7, 141n291
Kuzari (Halevi). *See* Judah Halevi
Koestler, Arthur, 104

La sacra scrittura (Sacred Scripture) (Lanci), 108
Laban, 26
Lachish Letters, 24
Lanci, Michelangelo, 107; *Chronicles (Paralipomeni alla Illustrazione della Sagra Scrittura Monumenti Fenico-Assirii ed Egiziana)*, 109; *Letter on the Interpretation of Egyptian Hieroglyphics, Addressed to Monsieur Prisse of Avennes (Lettre sur l'interprétation des Hiéroglyphes Égyptiens, adressée à M. Prisse d'Avennes)*, 110; *Sacred Scripture (La sacra scrittura)*, 108
Lante, Louis Marie, 115
Lecha Dodi (Alkabetz). *See* Alkabetz
Leeser, Isaac, 126n71
Le Thrésor des Prophéties de l'Univers (Postel), 115, 144n355
Lerner, Gerda, 89
Leroi-Gourhan, André, 119n26

Letter on the Interpretation of Egyptian Hieroglyphics, Addressed to Monsieur Prisse of Avennes (*Lettre sur l'interprétation des Hiéroglyphes Égyptiens, adressée à M. Prisse d'Avennes*) (Lanci), 110
letters of Hebrew alphabet: as male and female, 56. *See also* alef; bet; heh; *matres lectionis*
letters of Israel as anagram, 129n103
Lévi-Strauss, Claude, 119n26
Leviticus, x, 30, 129n103
Light of the Intellect (*Or ha-Sekhel*). *See* Abulafia.
Lion Man (*Löwenmensch*), 15
Louvre, 24
Löwenmensch, (Lion Man), 15
l'shem yichud, 82
Lurianic Kabbalah (Isaac Luria), 80, 81, 83–86, 89
Luther, Martin, 4

Maacah, 118
Ma'aseh Bereishit (Workings of Creation), 47, 57
Ma'aseh Merkabah (Workings of the Chariot), 47, 57
Mackey, Albert Gallatin, 113–15
magic, 45, 52, 70
Magid, Shaul, 142n309
Maimonides (Moses ben Maimon), 57–62, 64–65, 94; and Azriel, 65; calendar of, 72–73; and Einstein, 104; and Kabbalists, 81; and Gikatilla, 70; *Guide for the Perplexed*, 57–60; and text, 98
Mainz (Germany), 51, 54
Malabari (Indian Jews), 50
Man O' War (*Ish Milchamah*), 31, 123n68
Manasseh, King, 118n14

Marduk, 10, 31
Martin, Raymund: *Dagger of Faith against the Moors and the Jews* (*Pugio fidei adversus Mauros et Judaeos*), 4
Masons, 107, 113m115, 144n357; and Lanci, 115; and Mackey, 113–15; and Pius IX, 109–110; and Roman Catholic Church, 107; *Symbolism of Freemasonry* (Mackey), 113–14; Society of Freemasons, 107
Masoretes (*Ba'alei Masorah*), 3, 127n77
Masters of THE NAME (*Ba'alei Shem*): names of, 85, 140n289
Masters of the Tradition. *See* Masoretes
matres lectionis, 23, 121n47, 125n71, 127n71
meditation, 51–52, 65, 68, 84
Menachem Mendel of Vitebsk, 140n286
meneqet, 126n71
merism, 96
Mesha Stele (Moabite Stone), 24, 28
Messiah, 46, 56, 79, 82, 83, 87, 122n53
Messianic: age, 56, 73, 79, 82; fervor, 72; tendencies, 136n232; uprising, 44
Mesopotamia, x; civilizations of, 10; dual-gender gods of, 10–13; hybrids of, 14; languages of, 14; myths of, 13, 15–16
mezuzah, 5
mikvah, 84–85, 87, 140n286
Miriam, 34, 125n71, 128n88
mishkal, 139n279
Mishnah, 25, 47
Mitnagdim ("Opponents" of the Hasidim), 88
mitzvah, 79

INDEX

Mizrachi (Eastern) Jews, 50
Moabite Stone (Mesha Stele), 24, 28
modernity, 38, 96, 103, 105–6
Mordechai, 17, 32, 126n71
Moreh BeEtzbah (Azulai), 133n162
Moses: addressing God in feminine, 126n71; and Ezra, 30; Lanci's view of, 111; mystical union, 88; the name, 8, 35, 121n38; names of family members, 34–35; nursing father, 17; revelation to, 19, 28, 38, 59, 83; reverse reading by, 66; typology, 26
Moses ben Kalonymus of Lucca, 51
Moses ben Maimon. *See* Maimonides
Moses ben Nahman. *See* Nachmanides
Moses Chaim Ephraim of Sudylkow, 85, 140n288
Mount Mountain, 35
Mount Sinai, 28; as Horeb, 35, 128n99
Muslims: Almohad, 54, 57, 72; Almoravid, 72; Arabian, 131n136; Berber, 72; Sufi, 52; Umayyad, 72

Nabu, 31
Nachmanides (Moses ben Nahman), 67–68, 72
names of God: 72 three-letter, 5; Elohim, 36–37, 69, 108, 117n5, 118n13; Hu-Hi, ix, 8, 22, 23–24, 66, 68; HWHY, 66; Jehovah, ix, 2–4, 114; Yahweh, ix, 4, 18, 21, 25; YHWH, ix, 1, 3, 6, 8, 12, 19–23, 25, 36–37, 48, 66, 70, 82, 84–85; Yod Heh Vov Heh, 8, 55, 77. *See also,* trigrammaton, Tetragrammaton

Name of Ra (story), 20
Narmer, Pharaoh, 13
nasi (title), 46
Nathan, 7
Nebuchadnezar, King, 29, 31
Nehardea, 46
New York Historical Society, 115
New York Times, 8
Nicholas of Cusa: *coincidentia oppositorum*, 65
Noah, 26; God's command to, 76; her tent, 32–33, 124n71; sons of, 35, 125n71; wife of, 34
nomen proprium, 58
North African Jews, 50
Numbers, Book of, 30
nurse: God as, 120n27; king as, 17; *meneqet*, 126n71; miracle of man as, 120n27; Mordechai as, 17, 32, 126n71; *ohmen*, 126n71; *tithenos* 120n27. *See also* nursing father; nursing kings
nursing-father, 17, 32, 120n27, 126n71
nursing-kings, 17, 32, 126n71

ohmen, 126n71
ohr makif and *ohr p'nini*, 89
Or ha-Sekhel (Light of the Intellect). *See* Abulafia
Origen, 48–49
Oshaya, 46, 94
Otzar Eden HaGanuz, 136n218

palindromes, 59
Paralipomeni alla Illustrazione della Sagra Scrittura Monumenti Fenico-Assirii ed Egiziana (Lanci), 109
pardes, 67
Passover, 29, 85, 106, 123n58, 140n288

165

patriarch, office of, 45–46
patriarchy, 102, 123n67
Pentateuch, 30. *See also* individual books: Genesis, Exodus, Leviticus, Numbers, Deuteronomy
Perush Shem shel Arba Otiyyot. *See* Explanation of the Four-Lettered Name
Petrarch, 54
Pew Research Center, 97
Pharaoh's daughter, 35
pharaohs. *See* Akhenaten, Amenhotep III, Hatshepsut, Khafre, Narmer, Rameses II, Tuthmosis II
Pius IX, pope, 109. See also *Qui Pluribus*
Pinchas bar Chama, 45
Pinchas ben Shmuel (high priest), 44
Pinchas of Koretz, 140n286
Polen, Nehemiah: *The Holy Fire*, 92
popes: mid-thirteenth century, 72; Benedict XVI, 144n357; Clement XII, 144n357; Pius IX, 109; Sixtus IV, 144n355
Porchetus de Salvatici: *Victory against Jews* (*Victoria contra Judaeos*), 4
Postel, Guillaume: *The Treasure of the Prophecies of the Universe* (*Le Thrésor des Prophéties de l'Univers*), 115
postmodernity, 103
Prayer of Love, 87
priests (kohanim), ix, 1–2, 20–22, 24–26, 31, 33, 41–44, 52, 122n54. *See also* high priests
priestly blessing, 24, 44
proairetism, 128n79
pronouns, 59, 60, 68; Abulafia on Hebrew spelling of, 69; Maimonides on Arabic, 59;

THE NAME composed of, 96; Lanci on, 115
Provence (France), 53, 62–64, 66
Pugio fidei adversus Mauros et Judaeos (*Dagger of Faith against the Moors and the Jews*) (Raymund Martin), 4
Psalm 29, 19
Ptolemy II, 117n4
Pumbedita, 46, 48, 52

qere and *ketiv*, 33
qere perpetuum, 127n77
Qui pluribus, On Faith and Religion (Pius IX): 109, 144n342

rabbi (title), 44
Rainey, Anson, 18
Rameses II, Pharaoh, 120n29
Rashi: on alternative names, 129n103; on Elohim treated as singular, 108; on midrash of Moses uttering THE NAME, 131n129; on Moses addressing God in feminine, 126n71; on use of THE NAME to create life, 46
Ratzinger, Joseph. *See* Benedict XVI
Rav Zera: receives human being created with THE NAME, 48; bridal song sung to, 132n146
Rava: creates human being with THE NAME, 48
Razei Torah, 47
reading of Torah, public. See *qere and ketiv*
Rebecca, 34, 129n103; as young man, 32, 124n71
Reconquista, 72
Redford, Donald, 18
Resh Galuta, title. *See* exilarch.
Rome, 53
Romaniote (Greek Jews), 50
Rouen (France), 54

INDEX

Ruth, Book of: greeting with THE NAME, 25

Saadiah Gaon, 51
Sabbath Queen. See *Shabbat ha-Malka*
sacred coupling. See *zivvuga kadisha*
sacred marriage. See *hieros gamos*
Sacred Scripture (La sacra scrittura) (Lanci), 108
Samael, 79, 92
Samuel bar Nachman, 40
Sanctification of the New Moon. See *Kiddush ha-Chodesh*
Sanctification [prayer] of Orphans. See *Kaddish Yatom*
Sanhedrin, 44
Sanseverino, Conte Severino Servanzi Collio di, 115
šar pūhī, 122n54
Saragossa (Spain), 72
Sarah, 25, 34, 129n103
Sarai, 25–26, 34, 122n55
Scribal Culture (Toorn), 128n78
scribes: as apprentices 33; and cryptography, 6; and elite religion, 118n14; as initiates, 39; not to "correct" text, 124; scribal error, 32, 38; and tradition of oversize bet, 56; and trigrammaton, 23; and innovation of vowels, 22. *See also* Ben Sira; Shaphan; Ezra ha-Kohain; Masoretes; *qere* and *qetiv*
Second Temple: disagreement over spelling of "she" in period of, 124n71; destruction of, x, 2, 20, 42–44; Ezra pronounces THE NAME outside, 30; period, 1, 41, 49; rationale for not pronouncing THE NAME in period of, 21

Secret of God's Unity. See *Sod ha Yichud*
Secrets of the Torah (doctrine). See *Razei Torah*.
Sefad (Israel), 78
Sefardi (Spanish) Jews, 50
Sefer ha-Bahir (Book of Bright Light), 53–57, 61, 63–64, 95
Sefer ha-Brit (Book of the Covenant), 29–30
Sefer ha-Chokhmah (Book of Wisdom), 61
Sefer HaShem (Book of THE NAME), 61, 134n191
Sefer ha-Zohar. See Zohar (mystical work)
Book of Formation (Sefer Yetzirah), 46, 51, 55, 131n133, 131n140
sefirot, 55
Semites, 35. *See also* Shem (Noah's son)
Semitic deities, 19
Sen, Amartya, 104
Septuagint, 2–3, 117n4, 120n27, 126n71, 127n73
Seville (Spain), 78
Sex and World Peace (Hudson), 102
Sha'are Orah (Gates of Light) (Gikatilla): 69–71
Shabbat ha-Malka, 80
Shabbatai Tzvi, 82, 85
Shaphan, 28
Shapira, Kalonymus Kalman, 90–93
Sharabi, Sar Shalom, 83, 141n293
Shasu, x, 18
shekhinah (God's presence), 55
Shekhinah (female aspect of God), 55, 63, 83, 88, 141n296, 141n300
Shem (Noah's son), 35, 125n71. *See also* Noah
shem gadol, 139n281
shem katan, 139n281

167

INDEX

Shem Tov de Leon, Moses ben, 71.
    See also Zohar (mystical
    work)
shem tov (God's good name), 71
Shema, 66, 76, 86
Shephatiah Ba'al Shem, 51
Shimon bar Yochai, 73, 76
Shimon ha-Tzaddik (high priest,
    Simon the Just), 1–2, 41
Shmuel b. Nachmani, 48
shuckling, 87–89, 141n295
Siddur Kavvanot Ha-RaShash, 84
Simon the Just, (high priest, Shimon
    ha-Tzaddik), 1–2, 41
Sitrei Torah, 47
Sixtus IV (pope), 144n355
Smith, William Robertson, 19
Sod ha Yichud, 62
Soleb, 18–19, 41, 95, 120n29
Solomon, King, 12; Temple of,
    28–29
sovev and *mimalei*, 89
Spain, x, 50; Abulafia of, 68–69;
    Andalusia, forced
    conversions in, 54; Bachya
    ben Asher of, 77; Berber
    sacking of Córdoba, 72;
    expulsion from, 78–79;
    Gikatilla of, 70; golden
    age of, 71–72; Granada
    massacre, 54; Spanish
    Inquisition, 78; Kabbalistic
    teachings reach, 64;
    Kabbalists of Gerona,
    64–67; Maimonides of, 57;
    Nachmanides of, 67–86;
    Moses ben Shem Tov de
    Leon of, 71, 73; *Reconquista*,
    72; Seville massacre, 78;
    Toledo riots, 78. See also
    Zohar (mystical work)
Spanish (Sefardi), Jews, 50
    Sperling, S. David, 7
Speyer (Germany), 54

Sphinx, 4
sprachbund, 119n22
Standing Prayer. See *Amidah*
substitute king. See *šar pūhi*
substitute names for God: *Adonai*,
    2–3, 117n5, 121n38;
    Dominus, 2,3; *Kurios*
    (*Kýrios*), 2–3; Lord, x, 2–3
Sudan, 18, 120n29
Sufi saints, 52
Sumeria, 10, 13, 15, 22, 89, 118n14,
    119n22
Supplication. See *Tachanun*
Sura, 46
sovev and *mimalei*, 89
sword verses: Christian, 31; Jewish,
    123n68; Muslim, 31

Tachanun (Supplication), 42
Talmud, 1, 25, 30, 38, 42, 46–49,
    51–52, 55, 67, 73, 80, 82, 100
Tamar, as including male and
    female, 56
TaNaKh. See Hebrew Bible.
Tarfon, 44
Taylor, G. H. Parke: *Yahweh: The
    Divine Name in the Bible*, 21
Tel Aviv (Israel), 91
Ten Commandments, as containing
    male and female, 56
Ten Lost Tribes of Israel, 28
Tetragrammaton: frequency
    of transmission, 2;
    transmission over water
    61–62, 134n191. See also
    names of God
therianthropy, 119n25
theriocephaly, 119n25
three-letter name of God (YHW).
    See trigrammaton
theophoric names, 25
Tiamat, 16, 31, 119n20
Tiao Jin Jiao (Chinese Jews), 50
tikkun (repair), 139n279

Tikkun (text), 127n77
tithenos, 120n27
Titus, 71
Tiglath-Pileser III, King 31
Tocqueville, Alexis de, 111
Toldot Ya'akov Yosef, 141n298
Toledo (Spain), 78
Toorn, Karel van der, 33
Torah. *See* Pentateuch
"Torah Insights." *See* "Holy Fire" (Shapira)
Torquemada, Tomás de, 79
Trawniki, 92
Treasure of the Prophecies of the Universe (Postel), 115, 144n355
Tretyakov Gallery, 115
trigrammaton (YHW): at Soleb, 18; at Elephantine Island, 19; change to tetragrammaton, 23–26
Tuthmosis II, Pharaoh, 17, 35
Tyndale, William. *See* King James Bible
Tzippori (Israel), 45

Ugarit, 23, 118n14
unifications. *See yichudim*
Union Prayerbook for Jewish Worship, 88
unity of opposites, 41. *coincidentia oppositorum*, 65; *ha-achdut hashvaah*, 65
unification of THE NAME. *See yichud HaShem*

Vargas, Francesco, 108
Vatican, xi; bans Lanci's *Paralipomeni*, 109; bans Lanci's *Letter to Monsieur Prisse*, 111; and Freemasons, 115; and Lanci, 107, 110; suppresses Lanci's *La sacra scritura*, 108. *See also* popes; Lanci
versio vulgate, Vulgate, 2–3
Victoria contra Judaeos (Porchetus), 4
Victory against the Jews (Porchetus), 4
Vidas, Eliyahu de, 81, 139n278
Vilna Gaon, 141n291
Vital, Chaim, 81
vowels: Hebrew lacked indicators for, 124n71; innovation of, 22; Masoretes' marks for, 3; and matres lectionis, 23; of THE NAME, per Lanci, 112; of THE NAME, per Halevi and ibn Ezra, 121n47; mnemonics for Adonai, 3; and the name Jehovah, 3

wave-particle duality, 104
Wellhausen, Julius, 19, 36, 120n36, 130n111
"Who is He? He is She" (Sameth), 8
Whybray, R. N.: *The Making of the Pentateuch*, 37
Wilbur, Ken, 104
Wilkinson, Robert, 4, 121n37
Wolfson, Elliot, 137n252
Workings of Creation (*Ma'aseh Bereishit*), 47, 57
Workings of the Chariot (*Ma'aseh Merkabah*), 47, 57
Worms (Germany), 54, 61
writing: 14, 23. Assyrian block script, 30; *boustrophedon*, 122m48; hieroglyphics, 22; Paleo-Hebrew, 30; Phoenician, 22; 30; Sumerian cuneiform, 22

Yaakov Yosef of Polnoye, 87. *See also Toldot Ya'akov Yosef*

INDEX

Yah: in Elijah, 122n53; first syllable of Yahweh, 25; Luria's meditation on, 84; Lanci on, 109; meaning "she," 122n53; in theophoric names, 25, 122n53; wordplay in Polanya, 91

Yahweh, ix, 4, 18, 21, 25. *See also* names of God

Yannai, 80

Yavneh, 43–44

Yehuda (rabbi), 73

Yehuda Halevi. *See* Halevi

Yehudah he-Hasid (Judah ben Samuel, Judah the Pious), 60–62, 64, 66, 94

Yemen, 50

yichud HaShem, 81

yichudim, 81, 139n279

Yochanan, 48

Yochanan ben Zakkai, 44, 131n140

Yocheved, 34

Yod Heh Vov Heh, 8, 55, 77. *See also* names of God

Yom Kippur: THE NAME pronounced on, 2, 41; of 1939, 92

yordei merkavah, 132n142

Yose, 30, 76

Yosef (rabbi), 120n27, 123n65

YHW. *See* trigrammaton

YHWH, ix, 1, 3, 6, 8, 12, 19–23, 25, 36–37, 48, 66, 70, 82, 84–85. *See also* names of God

Zaphenath-Paneah, 34

Zera, 132n146

zivvuga kadisha, 74

Zohar (biblical character), 129n103

Zohar (mystical work), 55; and androgynous adam, 75, 137n252; authorship of, 73, 137n238; appearance in Spain, 71; backwards writing in, 76; dual-gender God made normative through, 5; and fluidity of male and female, 74–75; God's aspects pining for reunion in, 95; in Latin, 115; not to be read literally, 74, 98; popularity of, 73; and sacred coupling of Holy Mother and Holy Father, 74; and Shema, 76; studied above all other texts, 83, 133n162; and prayer, 76; unification of Moses and God in, 88, 141n300; and unifications, 81; and unity of male and female, 75

Index of Quotations from the Hebrew Bible

Genesis

1:5	63	17:5	25
1:9	135n194	17:15	25
1:27	125n71	20:5	124n71
2:22	40	21:31	121n38
3:12	123n71	22:14	121n38
3:20	40	24:2–7	128n97
4:26	129n103	24:14	124n71
5:2	40	24:16	124n71
5:32	129n101	24:21–32	128n97
6:10	129n101	24:28	124n71
7:7	128n92	24:34–53	128n97
7:13	128n92, 129n101	24:55	124n71
7:16	128n92	24:57	124n71
7:18	128n92	24:61	128n97
7:23	138n260	25:25–26	121n38
9:18	129n101	26:20	121n38
9:21	124n71	26:25	124n71
10:1	129n101	26:34	129n103
10:2	129n101	27:36	138n262
10:6	129n101	28:9	129n103
10:21	125n71, 129n101	28:11	128n83
11:9	121n38	28:19	129n103
12:1	128n82	29:16	125n71
12:5	128n82	31:47	128n98
12:8	124n71	31:49	128n98
13:3	124n71	32:29	121n38, 128n80
15:2	128n96	32:30	128n80, 128n94
16:13	126n71	32:31	121n38
		34:3–4	125n71
		34:12	125n71

Genesis (continued)

35:7	128n84, 129n103
35:10	128n80
35:14	128n80
35:15	129n103
35:18	128n100
35:21	124n71
36:2	129n103
36:3	129n103
36:24	129n103
37:30	125n71
37:35	128n93
38:3	138n261
38:25	124n71
42:11	136n217
46:10	129n103
46:13	129n103
41:45	128n81
48:14	127n76
49:1	121n43

Exodus

2:1	128n85, 131n129
2:4	128n87
2:5–10	128n95
2:7–8	128n87
2:10	121n38
2:16	128n89
2:18	128n90
3:1	128n91, 128n99
3:14	19, 59
4:18	128n91
6:3	129n103
6:20	128n86
15:20	125n71, 128n88
15:23	121n38
16:7–8	136n217
17:7	121n38
17:16	128n99
20:8	56
33:8	124n71

Leviticus

1:1	129n103
14:8	124n71
16:30	134n191

Numbers

5:13–14	124n71
6:24–25	24
6:27	56
10:29	128n91
11:3	121n38
11:10	124n71
11:12	17, 120n27, 126n71
11:15	126n71
13:6	129n103
20:22–29	129n102
26:13	129n103
26:24	129n103
26:59	128n88
32:32	136n217

Deuteronomy

5:12	56
6:4	66, 118n19
22:15–29	125n71
32:13	127n71
32:16	127n71
32:18	127n71
32:39	140n287
33:2	128n99
34:10	125n71

First Kings

15: 1–14	118n14
16:33	118n14
17:15	123n71
18:19	118n14

INDEX OF QUOTATIONS FROM THE HEBREW BIBLE

Second Kings

21:7	118n14
22:8	122n57
22:3–23:27	122n56

Isaiah

26:4	25
30:33	123n71
41:23	69, 136n218
49:23	17, 126n71
60:16	126n71

Jeremiah

11:21	127n76

Ezekiel

48:35	48

Joel

3:5	25

Amos

2:7	124n71

Jonah

2:1–2	127n71

Psalms

16:8	70
19:13	33
21:9	6
22:23	25
29:5	19
29:9	19
32:7	76
68:5	25, 109
73:16	123n71
82:1	118n13
91:14	70
104:2	68
118:6	109
118:22	108
119:18	33

Proverbs

3:6	86
25:11	64
27:6	126n71

Job

31:11	123n71
23:13	135n198

The Song of Songs

1:4	132n144

Ruth

2:4	25
4:16	126n71

Ecclesiastes

5:8	123n71

Esther

2:7	17

Daniel

7:9	132n143

Nehemiah

8:8	127n76

INDEX OF QUOTATIONS FROM THE HEBREW BIBLE

First Chronicles

29:16	123n71

Second Chronicles

11:20–22	118n14
15:16	118n14
34:3	122n56

About the Author

Named "one of America's most inspiring rabbis" by *The Forward* (inaugural list, 2013), Rabbi Mark Sameth (he/him/his) is featured in Jennifer Berne and R. O. Blechman's *God: 48 Famous and Fascinating Minds Talk about God* (Running Press). His essays appear in books published by Jewish Lights, CCAR Press, Jossey Bass, and New Paradigm Matrix and in *Reform Judaism Magazine*, *Journal of Jewish Education*, *CCAR Journal*, and the *New York Times* ("Is God Transgender?" Op-Ed, August 12, 2016).

www.ingramcontent.com/pod-product-compliance
Lightning Source LLC
Chambersburg PA
CBHW071231170426
43191CB00032B/1310